PREFACE

1. Scope

This publication provides guidelines for planning and conducting detainee operations. It outlines responsibilities, discusses organizational options, and provides command and control considerations across the range of military operations.

2. Purpose

This publication has been prepared under the direction of the Chairman of the Joint Chiefs of Staff (CJCS). It sets forth joint doctrine to govern the activities and performance of the Armed Forces of the United States in joint operations and provides the doctrinal basis for interagency coordination and for US military involvement in multinational operations. It provides military guidance for the exercise of authority by combatant commanders and other joint force commanders (JFCs) and prescribes joint doctrine for operations, education, and training. It provides military guidance for use by the Armed Forces in preparing their plans. It is not the intent of this publication to restrict the authority of the JFC from organizing the force and executing the mission in a manner the JFC deems most appropriate to ensure unity of effort in the accomplishment of the overall objective.

3. Application

a. Joint doctrine established in this publication applies to the Joint Staff, commanders of combatant commands, subordinate unified commands, joint task forces, subordinate components of these commands, the Services, and combat support agencies. This publication also provides information to US Government departments and agencies, the National Guard Bureau, multinational partners, intergovernmental organizations, and nongovernmental organizations.

b. The guidance in this publication is authoritative; as such, this doctrine will be followed except when, in the judgment of the commander, exceptional circumstances dictate otherwise. If conflicts arise between the contents of this publication and the contents of Service publications, this publication will take precedence unless the CJCS, normally in coordination with the other members of the Joint Chiefs of Staff, has provided more current and specific guidance. Commanders of forces operating as part of a multinational (alliance or coalition) military command should follow multinational doctrine and procedures ratified by the United States. For doctrine and procedures not ratified by the United States, commanders should evaluate and follow the multinational command's doctrine and procedures, where applicable and consistent with US law, regulations, and doctrine.

For the Chairman of the Joint Chiefs of Staff:

DAVID L. GOLDFEIN, Lt Gen, USAF
Director, Joint Staff

- **Expands discussion of biometric capabilities.**

- **Enhances discussion of humane treatment.**

- **Adds reference to Article 75 of the First Additional Protocol to the Geneva Conventions.**

- **Revises terminology, taxonomy, and definitions for unlawful enemy combatant, unprivileged belligerent, detainee, and detainee operations.**

- **Removes discussion of strategic communication.**

- **Expands the discussion on public affairs responsibilities.**

- **Adds a discussion pertaining to internment serial numbers.**

- **Adds a discussion on field reporter number.**

- **Modifies the discussion on the International Committee of the Red Cross.**

- **Revises naming convention of internment facilities.**

- **Clarifies distinction between detainee transfer and detainee release.**

Intentionally Blank

TABLE OF CONTENTS

APPENDIX

GLOSSARY

FIGURE

EXECUTIVE SUMMARY
COMMANDER'S OVERVIEW

- **Provides an introduction on detainee operations policy, legal considerations, and detainee categories**

- **Discusses the roles and responsibilities for detainee operations**

- **Describes the planning and conduct of detainee operations**

- **Covers capture and initial detention and screening of detainees**

Introduction

Detainee operations is a broad term that encompasses the capture, initial detention and screening, transportation, treatment and protection, housing, transfer, and release of the wide range of persons who could be categorized as detainees.

During the conduct of military operations, members of the Armed Forces of the United States must possess the capability to plan, execute, and support detainee operations during military operations. Regardless of the type of military operation, the potential requirement to detain individuals (hereafter referred to as detainees) exists, and US forces must treat all detainees humanely and be prepared to properly control, maintain, protect, and account for detainees in accordance with applicable US law, the law of war, and applicable US policy. These standards also apply to all non-Department of Defense (DOD) personnel as a condition of permitting access to internment facilities or to detainees under DOD control.

Policy

Department of Defense Directive 2310.01E, *The Department of Defense Detainee Program,* establishes overarching DOD detainee policy. Inhumane treatment of detainees is prohibited by the Uniform Code of Military Justice, domestic and international law, and DOD policy. All DOD personnel or DOD contractor personnel will immediately report incidents through their chain of command or supervision for ultimate transmission to appropriate US authorities or other appropriate authorities.

Legal Considerations

US detainee operations must comply with the law of war during all armed conflicts, no matter how such conflicts are characterized, and in all other military operations. The law of war regulates the conduct of armed hostilities and occupation and encompasses all international law for the conduct of hostilities binding on the US or its individual citizens, including treaties and international agreements to which the US is a party, and applicable customary international law.

Detainee Categories

The word "detainee" includes any person captured, detained, or otherwise under the control of DOD personnel. The detainee categories are:

- **Belligerent.** In general, a person who is engaged in hostilities against the US or its multinational partners during an armed conflict. The term belligerent includes both privileged belligerent and unprivileged enemy belligerent.

- **Retained Personnel.** An individual who is described by Article 28 of the Geneva Convention for the Amelioration of the Condition of the Wounded and Sick in Armed Forces in the Field and Article 33 of the Geneva Convention Relative to the Treatment of Prisoners of War and who is in the custody or control of DOD.

- **Civilian Internee.** Any civilian, including those described by Article 4 of the Geneva Convention Relative to the Protection of Civilian Persons in Time of War, who is in the custody or control of DOD during an armed conflict or occupation, such as those held for imperative reasons of security or protection.

Roles and Responsibilities

Combatant Commanders

Combatant commanders are responsible for the DOD Detainee Program.

Subordinate Joint Force Commanders and Component Commanders

The Joint Force Commander may assign a commander of detainee operations to provide focused attention to detainee operations.

Subordinate joint force commanders (JFCs) have the overall responsibility for the planning and conduct of detainee operations in their assigned joint operations area (JOA). JFCs will ensure detainee operations in their JOA comply with international law of war and the applicable policy and doctrine. JFCs will ensure that persons captured or detained by US Armed Forces are safely handed over to a detainee collection point (DCP) as soon as practical. Commanders at all levels will ensure that all categories of detainees are accounted for and humanely treated, and that collection, evacuation, internment, transfers, release, and repatriation of detainees are conducted in accordance with applicable law, policy, and doctrine.

Commander, Detainee Operations

The commander, detainee operations (CDO) is typically responsible for all detention facility and interrogation operations in the JOA. The JFC typically assigns the CDO the following responsibilities: Exercise operational control over all assigned and attached forces, detention facilities, and joint interrogation and debriefing centers (JIDCs), regardless of location within the JOA. Provide for the humane treatment of detainees. Immediately report all allegations of maltreatment and/or abuse of detainees. Thoroughly investigate and immediately report all substantiated allegations through designated command channels. Coordinate all reporting requirements between military police detention battalions and the theater detainee reporting center.

Detention Facility Commander

The detention facility commander is the commander responsible for all detention facility operations.

Joint Interrogation and Debriefing Center Commander

The JIDC commander and/or chief is the officer responsible to the CDO for all matters relating to interrogation, intelligence collection and reporting, and interaction with other agencies involved in the intelligence and/or evidence gathering process.

Human Intelligence Collectors, Debriefers, and Interpreters

Within the intelligence directorate of a joint staff, the joint force counterintelligence and human intelligence staff element officer and collection manager is normally assigned the responsibility for the technical control, support, and deconfliction of all counterintelligence and human intelligence (HUMINT) activities within the JOA. This includes the identification of information requirements, coordination and assignment of interrogators, intelligence analysts, and HUMINT collectors to any JIDCs in the JOA.

Planning and Conducting Detainee Operations

Detainee Operations Planning Considerations

JFCs should anticipate operational and logistical requirements well in advance of conducting detainee operations. Site selection for a detainee facility is critical and must incorporate a wide range of factors including logistical supportability, security, mitigation of escape attempts, and engineering aspects. Consideration should be given to the garrison support activities that support an operating base where detention facilities are located.

Other Considerations

Other planning considerations for detainee operations include force protection; logistics; property safekeeping and confiscation accountability; administrative processing and accountability; religious, intellectual, and physical activities; a mechanism for command interaction with the International Committee of the Red Cross and nongovernmental organizations and other similar organizations; and media requests.

Capture and Initial Detention and Screening of Detainees

Capture and Initial Screening

Once the capture of individuals has occurred, the proper identification and classification of those personnel is critical to the overall intelligence and detainee operations effort. Rapid collection of biometrics information from detainees is critical to ensuring their prompt identification, and is a crucial step that must be conducted as soon as possible after detention. The initial classification of a detainee may be based on unsupported statements or documentation accompanying the detainee. After a detainee is assigned to a facility, expect a continuing need for further classification.

Individuals captured or detained by US forces must be evacuated expeditiously through transit points to reach a detention facility in a secure area.

The **DCP** will support the rapid transfer of control from capturing forces to US military police or other approved units for custody and control. DCP should be located close to the area of actual operations for quick detainee evacuation, but also be situated in a safe, secure location for both detainees and the security force. Detainees should be transported from the DCP to the **detainee holding area (DHA)** as soon as practicable. Upon arrival at the DHA, HUMINT collectors will normally screen all arriving detainees to determine those suspected of possessing information of immediate tactical value. Detainees will be transported to a **theater detention facility (TDF)** based on intelligence exploitation and transportation availability, at which point they will normally be assigned an internment serial number. A TDF is an improved, semipermanent, or permanent facility that can hold detainees until they are released or until it is determined that out-of-theater evacuation is necessary.

Secondary Screening and Confirmation	The tactical commander/leader has responsibilities to properly handle and prepare detainees for subsequent transfer to a DHA or TDF. Additionally, detention facility commanders and interrogation commanders must have clearly defined secondary screening and confirmation policies and procedures to receive detainees from point of capture units.
Detainee Movement Planning	The primary considerations for detainee escort missions are the security of the conveyance, the safety of all US resources, and the protection of the detainees. The coordination for the transportation of detainees is the responsibility of the detaining power and is a task that must be performed by military personnel.
Detainee Disposition	A detainee disposition describes the intended status of a detainee's liberty, confinement, or fate upon release from DOD control. A disposition will be indicated on release or repatriation orders generated by the detainee reporting system.
Detainee Classification	The initial classification of a detainee may be based on unsupported statements or documentation accompanying the detainee. After a detainee is assigned to a facility, expect a continuing need for further classification. If the detainee's classification remains in doubt, a tribunal may be convened to determine the detainee's status.
Review and Approval Process	For transfer or release authority of US-captured detainees, the Secretary of Defense, or the Secretary of Defense's designee, will establish criteria for the transfer or release of detainees and communicate those criteria to all commanders operating within the theater.

CONCLUSION

This publication provides guidelines for planning and conducting detainee operations. It outlines responsibilities, discusses organizational options, and provides command and control considerations across the range of military operations.

Intentionally Blank

CHAPTER I
INTRODUCTION

> *"Maxim 109. Prisoners of war do not belong to the power for which they have fought; they are under the safeguard of honour and generosity of the nation that has disarmed them."*
>
> ***The Military Maxims of Napoleon*, 1827, Burnod**

1. Background

During the conduct of military operations, members of the Armed Forces of the United States must possess the capability to plan, execute, and support detainee operations during military operations. Regardless of the type of military operation, the potential requirement to detain individuals (hereafter referred to as detainees) exists, and US forces must treat all detainees humanely and be prepared to properly control, maintain, protect, and account for detainees in accordance with (IAW) applicable US law, the law of war, and applicable US policy. The challenges of today's security environment and the nature of the enemy require clear operational and strategic guidance for detainee operations in a joint environment.

2. Policy

Department of Defense Directive (DODD) 2310.01E, *The Department of Defense Detainee Program,* establishes overarching Department of Defense (DOD) detainee policy. The directive requires humane treatment of all detainees during all armed conflicts, however characterized, and in all other military operations. The standards of treatment set forth in the directive apply to all DOD components and DOD contractors assigned to or supporting the DOD components engaged in, conducting, participating in, or supporting detainee operations. These standards also apply to all non-DOD personnel as a condition of permitting access to internment facilities or to detainees under DOD control.

a. Because the treatment standard applies from the point of capture throughout detention, DOD personnel and contractor employees must receive training on detainee operations. Inhumane treatment of detainees is prohibited by the Uniform Code of Military Justice, domestic and international law, and DOD policy. Accordingly, there is no exception to or deviation from this humane treatment requirement.

b. All DOD personnel or DOD contractor personnel will immediately report incidents through their chain of command or supervision for ultimate transmission to appropriate US authorities or other appropriate authorities. Reports also may be made through other channels, such as the military police (MP), a judge advocate, or an inspector general, who will then forward a report through the appropriate chain of command. On-scene commanders shall ensure that measures are taken to preserve evidence of alleged violations pending investigation by appropriate authorities.

3. Legal Considerations

a. US detainee operations must comply with the law of war during all armed conflicts, no matter how such conflicts are characterized, and in all other military operations. The law of war regulates the conduct of armed hostilities and occupation and encompasses all international law for the conduct of hostilities binding on the US or its individual citizens, including treaties and international agreements to which the US is a party, and applicable customary international law.

b. The four Geneva Conventions of 1949 apply as a matter of international law to all military operations that qualify as international armed conflicts and cases of partial or total occupation. These treaties are intended to provide comprehensive humanitarian standards for the treatment of war victims without adverse distinction. Although often referred to collectively as the "Geneva Conventions," the specific treaties are:

(1) **Geneva Convention for the Amelioration of the Condition of the Wounded and Sick in Armed Forces in the Field (GWS).** This convention provides protection for members of the armed forces and other persons on the battlefield who are no longer actively participating in hostilities as the result of becoming wounded or sick. It requires humane treatment for wounded and sick personnel who fall into enemy hands, with an express requirement that such individuals be protected against pillage and ill treatment and provided necessary and adequate care. It also provides for the collection of human remains and the recording of interment locations, and prohibits the abuse of remains.

(2) **Geneva Convention for the Amelioration of the Condition of Wounded, Sick, and Shipwrecked Members of Armed Forces at Sea.** This convention requires the humane treatment and protection of members of the armed forces and other persons at sea who are wounded, sick, or shipwrecked. It also protects hospital ships and provides a procedure for burial at sea.

(3) The **Geneva Convention Relative to the Treatment of Prisoners of War (GPW).** This convention provides for the humane treatment of enemy prisoners of war (EPWs). It regulates the treatment of EPWs (care, food, clothing, medical care, and housing), discipline and punishment, labor and pay, external relations, representation, the international exchange of information, and the termination of captivity.

(4) The **Geneva Convention Relative to the Protection of Civilian Persons in Time of War (GC).** This convention deals with the protection of civilians who find themselves under the control of an enemy nation (normally during a period of belligerent occupation). It regulates the treatment of such civilians, including establishing procedures

> **The United States has chosen out of a sense of legal obligation to treat the principles set forth in Article 75 of the First Additional Protocol to the Geneva Conventions as applicable to any individual it detains in international armed conflicts.**

for the deprivation of liberty (arrest, internment, assigned residence), and it provides a legal framework for the relationship between civilians and the enemy authorities controlling them.

c. DODD 2310.01E, *The Department of Defense Detainee Program,* addresses legal issues regarding the reception, treatment, processing, and release of detainees. It includes DOD policy relative to the minimum standards of treatment for all detainees in the control of DOD personnel. IAW US law and DOD policy, Common Article 3 to the Geneva Conventions of 1949 establishes minimum standards for the humane treatment of all persons detained by the US, allied, and multinational forces during non-international armed conflicts. IAW with USG and DOD policy, the principles set forth in Article 75 of Additional Protocol I to the Geneva Conventions establishes minimum standards for the humane treatment of all persons detained by US forces during international armed conflicts. Common Article 3 prohibits at any time and in any place "violence to life and person, in particular murder of all kinds, mutilation, cruel treatment and torture; taking of hostages; outrages upon personal dignity, in particular humiliating and degrading treatment; the passing of sentences and the carrying out of executions without previous judgment pronounced by a regularly constituted court, affording all the judicial guarantees which are recognized as indispensable by civilized peoples."

d. Multi-Service issuance Army Regulation (AR) 190-8/Chief of Naval Operations Instruction (OPNAVINST) 3461.6/Air Force Instruction (AFI) 31-304/Marine Corps Order (MCO) 3461.1, *Enemy Prisoners of War, Retained Personnel, Civilian Internees and Other Detainees,* addresses legal considerations when conducting detainee operations.

4. Detainee Categories

The word "detainee" includes any person captured, detained, or otherwise under the control of DOD personnel (see Figure I-1). This does not include DOD personnel or DOD contractor personnel or other persons being held primarily for law enforcement purposes except where the US is the occupying power. As a matter of policy, all detainees will be treated as EPWs until the appropriate legal status is determined and granted by competent authority IAW the criteria enumerated in the GPW. Detaining officials must recognize that detained belligerents who have not satisfied the applicable criteria in the GPW are still entitled to humane treatment, IAW Common Article 3 of the GPW during non-international armed conflicts, and the principles set forth in Article 75 of Additional Protocol I to the Geneva Conventions during international armed conflicts. The inhumane treatment of detainees is prohibited and is not justified by the stress of combat or deep provocation.

a. **Belligerent.** In general, a person who is engaged in hostilities against the US or its multinational partners during an armed conflict. The term belligerent includes both privileged belligerent and unprivileged enemy belligerent. Belligerents, who are entitled to protections under the GPW, include members of the regular armed forces of a state party to the conflict; militia, volunteer corps, and organized resistance movements belonging to a state party to the conflict, which are under responsible command, wear a fixed distinctive sign recognizable at a distance, carry their arms openly, and abide by the laws of war; and members of regular armed forces who profess allegiance to a government or an authority not recognized by the detaining power.

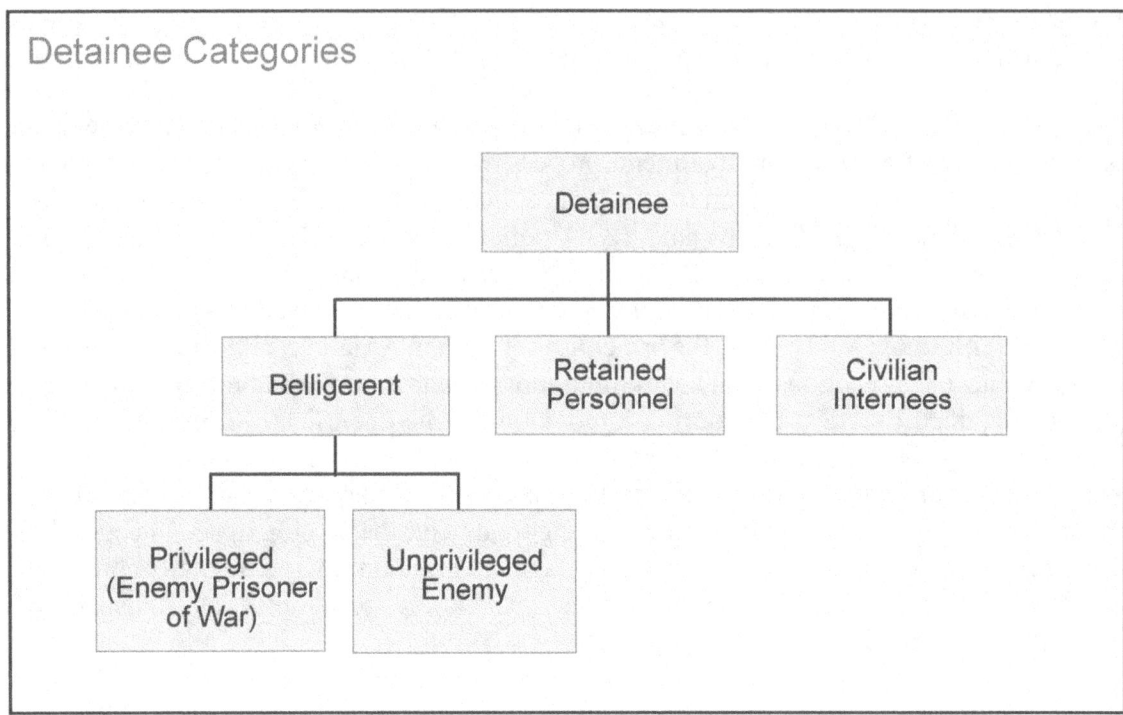

Figure I-1. Detainee Categories

(1) Privileged belligerents are EPWs upon capture, and are entitled to combatant immunity for their lawful pre-capture war-like acts. They may be prosecuted for violations of the law of war. If so prosecuted, they still retain their status as EPWs.

(2) Unprivileged enemy belligerents are belligerents who do not qualify for the distinct privileges of combatant status (e.g., combatant immunity). Examples of unprivileged belligerents are:

(a) Individuals who have forfeited the protections of civilian status by joining or substantially supporting an enemy non-state armed group in the conduct of hostilities, and

(b) Combatants who have forfeited the privileges of combatant status by engaging in spying, sabotage, or other similar acts behind enemy lines.

b. **Retained Personnel (RP).** An individual who is described by Article 28 of the GWS and Article 33 of the GPW and who is in the custody or control of DOD. Personnel who fall into the following categories: official medical personnel of the armed forces of the parties to the conflict, exclusively engaged in the search for, or the collection, transport, or treatment of wounded or sick, or in the prevention of disease, and staff exclusively engaged in the administration of medical units and establishments; chaplains attached to enemy armed forces; staff of the International Federation of Red Cross and Red Crescent Societies and that of other volunteer aid societies duly recognized and authorized by their governments to assist medical service personnel of their own armed forces, provided they are exclusively engaged in the search for, or the collection, transport or treatment of, the wounded or sick, or in the prevention of disease, and provided that the staff of such societies are subject to military laws and regulations.

c. **Civilian Internee (CI).** Any civilian, including those described by Article 4 of the GC, who is in the custody or control of DOD during an armed conflict or occupation, such as those held for imperative reasons of security or protection. Such individuals, unless they have committed acts for which they are considered unprivileged enemy belligerents, generally qualify for protected status IAW the GC, which also establishes procedures that must be observed when depriving such civilians of their liberty. CIs are to be accommodated separately from EPWs and persons deprived of liberty for any other reason.

Intentionally Blank

CHAPTER II
ROLES AND RESPONSIBILITIES

"A purely military emergency could give no excuse for disregarding International Law. Because victory is endangered, victory must not be pursued by breaking the law on the grounds of necessity, because the laws of warfare are supposed to rule over this conflict which is always connected with need and want."

Trial of German War Criminals, Nuremberg, 1946

1. Chairman of the Joint Chiefs of Staff

The CJCS is responsible for implementing the DOD Detainee Program and for assigning responsibilities to Joint Staff offices and directorates to ensure appropriate oversight of combatant command detainee operations, policies, and procedures, including ensuring operational exercises routinely test the capabilities of DOD components to conduct, participate in, and support detainee operations. Specific CJCS responsibilities related to detainee operations are promulgated in DODD 2310.01E, *The Department of Defense Detainee Program.*

2. Combatant Commanders

Combatant commanders (CCDRs) are responsible for the DOD Detainee Program. This includes ensuring compliance with applicable law, policy, and joint doctrine related to detainee operations. Specific CCDR responsibilities related to planning, execution, and oversight of combatant command detainee operations are promulgated in DODD 2310.01E, *The Department of Defense Detainee Program,* and Chairman of the Joint Chiefs of Staff Instruction (CJCSI) 3290.01, *Program for Detainee Operations.*

3. Subordinate Joint Force Commanders

Subordinate joint force commanders (JFCs) have the overall responsibility for detainee operations in their assigned joint operations area (JOA). JFCs will ensure detainee operations in their JOA comply with international law of war and the applicable policy and doctrine. JFCs will ensure that persons captured or detained by US Armed Forces are safely handed over to a detainee collection point (DCP) as soon as practical. JFCs must ensure the proper force structure to conduct detainee operations is included in any joint operational plans. Commanders at all levels will ensure that all categories of detainees are accounted for and humanely treated, and that collection, evacuation, internment, transfers, release, and repatriation of detainees are conducted IAW applicable law, policy, and doctrine. Additional specific responsibilities relating to detainee operations may be assigned to the JFC by the geographic combatant commander. The JFC may assign a commander, detainee operations (CDO), to provide focused attention to detainee operations.

4. Component Commanders

In addition to the roles and responsibilities of the subordinate JFC listed above, the component commanders identify conflicts between component doctrine and operational plans, policies, and procedures, and seek guidance through component command channels on effective deconfliction procedures.

5. Commander, Detainee Operations

The CDO is typically responsible for all detention facility and interrogation operations in the JOA. The CDO should have detainee operations experience and will normally be the senior MP commander. If the size and scope of the detainee operation warrants, the JFC may consider designating a general or flag officer as the CDO. The JFC typically assigns the CDO the following responsibilities:

a. Exercise operational control over all assigned and attached forces, detention facilities, and joint interrogation and debriefing centers (JIDCs), regardless of location within the JOA. JIDC non-detainee related activities should remain under the direction of the JFC and/or intelligence directorate of a joint staff.

b. Report directly to the JFC or designated Service or functional component commander on all detainee matters.

c. Ensure the development of detainee policies, procedures, orders, and directives for the JFC IAW applicable laws, regulations, and policies.

d. Provide for the humane treatment of detainees. Immediately report all allegations of maltreatment and/or abuse of detainees. Thoroughly investigate and immediately report all substantiated allegations through designated command channels.

e. Coordinate all reporting requirements between MP detention battalions and the theater detainee reporting center (TDRC).

f. Facilitate coordination between JIDC commander(s) and/or chiefs with the joint force counterintelligence and human intelligence staff element (J-2X).

g. Ensure all logistical requirements for detention facilities and JIDCs are determined and met. These logistical requirements range from initial setup of detention facilities to sustained operations throughout the life of a facility. Coordinate with J-2X on requirements for the interrogation facility to adequately address operational requirements.

h. Coordinate with J-2X (when established) to conduct human intelligence (HUMINT) and counterintelligence collection management efforts, and with the joint security office (when established) to conduct biometric collection management efforts.

i. Coordinate with appropriate commanders and staffs to disseminate JFC priorities for detainee operations throughout the JOA.

j. Obtain JFC's approval for external visit times and coordinate visits to detention facilities with the TDRC and joint visitor bureau.

k. Coordinate all International Committee of the Red Cross (ICRC) visits, and ensure the command responds to ICRC concerns, as necessary.

l. Ensure joint strategic exploitation center, JIDC commander, and the detention facility commander (DFC) responsibilities are clearly delineated. Coordinate all procedures in order to accomplish JIDC intelligence activities efficiently and accomplish security requirements effectively at all facilities, while treating all detainees humanely.

m. Ensure the issuance of internment serial numbers (ISNs) IAW current policies and procedures.

n. Establish, maintain, and supervise the detainee review process.

o. Coordinate with the JFC legal advisor for guidance in all matters of planning and execution of operations in order to maintain compliance with applicable laws and regulations.

p. Coordinate with the joint force surgeon (JFS) for guidance in all detainee medical care and health matters.

q. Coordinate with JFC postal staff for guidance relating to postal support for detainees.

r. Establish a plan to provide postal support to detainees when operationally feasible.

s. Ensure detainee release agreements to other nations, and the circumstances under which detainees are released to other nations, comply with US law and policy, and international law. For EPWs, if the nation that receives the EPWs fails to carry out the provisions of the GPW in any important respect, effective measures should be taken to correct the situation or the EPWs return shall be requested.

6. Detention Facility Commander

The DFC is the commander responsible for the execution of all detention facility operations. He or she is responsible, when assigned, to the CDO for all matters relating to detention facility operations, including security, law enforcement, administration, logistics, and other operations support requirements. A DFC's responsibilities normally include the following:

a. Ensure the humane treatment of detainees at all times and under all circumstances.

b. Establish detention facility standard operating procedures (SOPs) that ensure the detention operations mission is conducted IAW applicable US law and policy.

c. Ensure the safety, well-being, and training of all personnel operating the facility.

d. Ensure the effective management and distribution of logistic resources.

e. Ensure all detainee maltreatment allegations are immediately reported through appropriate command channels and corrective actions are initiated.

f. Ensure that all personnel are properly trained on the rules for the use of force; the law of land warfare, including the Geneva Conventions and all other applicable laws and policies; and that all personnel have an effective knowledge of the detention facility SOP.

g. Plan for and, when necessary, execute effective perimeter security of the detention facility, including personnel and material aspects and external response force operations and planning.

h. Assign escort guards for all detainee transportation entering or departing the facility.

i. Develop, along with the interrogation commander, procedures that include accountability and security of detainees during interrogation operations.

j. Coordinate force protection.

k. Ensure proper reporting of detainee accountability through the TDRC.

l. Conduct biometric collection and enrollment into the DOD biometric system of record for each detainee.

m. Coordinate with military criminal investigative organizations and legal agencies regarding evidentiary and other legal matters as required.

n. Coordinate with the civil-military operations center to facilitate interaction with intergovernmental organizations, nongovernmental organizations (NGOs), multinational forces, and other United States Government (USG) departments and agencies. For further information on civil-military operations, see Joint Publication (JP) 3-57, *Civil-Military Operations.*

o. Ensure operations security of all detention facilities' activities, security operations, support, and collection operations.

For further guidance on the responsibilities of the DFC, see AR 190-8/OPNAVINST 3461.6/AFI 31-304/MCO 3461.1, Enemy Prisoners of War, Retained Personnel, Civilian Internees and Other Detainees.

7. Joint Interrogation and Debriefing Center Commander

The JIDC commander and/or chief is the officer responsible to the CDO for all matters relating to interrogation, intelligence collection and reporting, and interaction with other agencies involved in the intelligence and/or evidence gathering process. The JIDC commander should be an intelligence officer and is normally responsible to:

a. Conduct interrogation operations IAW applicable US law and policy.

b. Coordinate with the DFC to ensure detainee operations do not set the conditions for interrogation operations. However, they may cooperate in responding to requests to facilitate interrogation operations, pursuant to DODD 3115.09, *DOD Intelligence Interrogations, Detainee Debriefings, and Tactical Questioning.*

c. Coordinate with the DFC for participation in base operations support including tenant unit force protection, interpreter support, and logistics.

d. Inform the CDO on interrogation operations.

e. Execute interrogation and debriefing operations according to priorities and guidance outlined by the J-2X.

f. Establish procedures to immediately report collected time-sensitive intelligence related to isolated or missing US or allied personnel to the joint intelligence operations center of the applicable geographic combatant commander.

For further information, see Department of Defense Instruction (DODI) 3115.10, Intelligence Support to Personnel Recovery, *and JP 3-50,* Personnel Recovery.

g. Coordinate detainee movement with the DFC to support interrogation operations.

h. Immediately report all allegations of maltreatment of detainees through the appropriate command channels IAW DOD policy.

8. Human Intelligence Collectors, Debriefers, and Interpreters

a. Within the intelligence directorate of a joint staff, the J-2X officer and collection manager is normally assigned the responsibility for the technical control, support, and deconfliction of all counterintelligence and HUMINT activities within the JOA. This includes the identification of information requirements, coordination and assignment of interrogators, intelligence analysts, and HUMINT collectors to any JIDCs in the JOA. The interrogation and debriefing of detainees is one of the most important counterintelligence and HUMINT collection activities conducted to support military operations because the exploitation of the detainee for time-sensitive tactical intelligence supports tactical, operational, and strategic requirements.

For further guidance on the roles and responsibilities of counterintelligence and HUMINT specialists supporting detainee operations, see DODD 3115.09, DOD Intelligence Interrogations, Detainee Debriefings, and Tactical Questioning, *JP 2-01.2,* Counterintelligence and Human Intelligence in Joint Operations, *and Field Manual (FM) 2-22.3,* Human Intelligence Collector Operations.

b. **Debriefers.** In most instances, detainees in DOD custody are interrogated, but qualified DOD debriefers are authorized to conduct debriefings of cooperative detainees IAW DODD 3115.09, *DOD Intelligence Interrogations, Detainee Debriefings, and Tactical*

> **NOTE:** As interrogation is deemed an inherently governmental function, no enemy prisoner of war, civilian internee, retained personnel, other detainee, or any other individual who is in the custody or under the effective control of the Department of Defense (DOD) or otherwise under detention in a DOD facility in connection with hostilities may be interrogated by contractor personnel unless the Secretary of Defense determines that the use of contract interrogators is vital to United States national security interests and waives the prohibition against their use for a period not to exceed 60 days.

Questioning. The use of debriefers to deal with cooperative detainees allows commanders to more efficiently utilize the limited number of available interrogators to conduct interrogations. DODD 3115.09, *DOD Intelligence Interrogations, Detainee Debriefings, and Tactical Questioning,* provides guidance on the use of debriefers.

(1) Authorized to utilize only direct questioning approach.

(2) Develop indicators for each intelligence requirement to support screening operations.

(3) Report information collected during debriefing operations through established HUMINT systems.

(4) Ensure all debriefing operations are implemented IAW applicable policy.

(5) A trained debriefer or trained interrogator may debrief a detainee.

c. **Interpreters.** Unless otherwise authorized by the JFC, only individuals with the proper training and appropriate level security clearance will be allowed within the confines of the facility to perform interpreter duties. Categories of contract interpreters include:

(1) **Category (CAT) I Linguists**—CAT I linguists do not possess a security clearance and are used for unclassified work. They can be local hires with an understanding of the English language or US citizens with an understanding of the target language. Those personnel that are hired in theater undergo a limited screening and are required to be re-screened on a scheduled basis. CAT I linguists will not be used for HUMINT collection operations.

(2) **CAT II Linguists**—CAT II linguists are US citizens who have native command of the target language and near-native command of the English language. These personnel undergo a screening process, which includes a national agency check. Upon favorable findings, these personnel are granted a Secret collateral clearance, the linguist category most used by HUMINT collectors.

(3) **CAT III Linguists**—CAT III linguists are US citizens who have native command of the target language and native command of the English language. These personnel undergo a screening process, which includes a special background investigation.

Upon favorable findings, these personnel are granted a Top Secret clearance. CAT III linguists are used mostly for high-ranking official meetings and by strategic collectors.

9. Joint Force Staff Elements

a. Civil Affairs Officer

(1) Recommends measures intended to enhance the level of cooperation between US forces and the detainee population.

(2) Assists the security force commander with control of detainees during emergencies.

(3) Serves as the coordinator between detainees and other agencies (e.g., military forces, humanitarian organizations, United Nations) as needed.

b. Military Information Support Personnel

(1) Assist the camp security forces by providing loudspeaker, audiovisual, and print support in regard to camp instructions in the target language(s).

(2) Provide a graduated response through loudspeakers in crisis situations prior to the use of nonlethal or lethal force.

(3) Provide cultural expertise on potential disputes or discipline problems due to social or cultural conflicts with or among detainees.

(4) Assist camp personnel in assessing and, if necessary, countering rumors, disinformation, and propaganda spread by detainees.

(5) Expose detainees to approved military information support operations (MISO) products relevant to new conditions they may face upon release and the behaviors expected of them upon release.

(6) Evaluate MISO products possessed by detainees.

(7) When applicable, build rapport with detainees through face-to-face communication and/or recreational activities.

c. Medical Officer or Surgeon

(1) Reports directly to the DFC with direct access to the CDO (as needed) and maintains a chain of command independent of the guard forces.

(2) Coordinates actions of medically qualified RP (individuals who satisfy the criteria for this status as established in the GWS). Provides first responder capability to the detainee population. Coordinates forward resuscitative care or higher capability.

(3) Advises the commander on medical and health-related issues. Coordinates for medical consultations with appropriate medical specialists and coordinates for transportation and escort of detainees to appointments, if required. Ensures medical information pertaining to the detainee's mental health condition and stability be included in the process for sharing medical information with the interrogation component.

(4) Coordinates with the civil affairs officer to ensure detainee medical concerns are being considered for possible presentation at the civil-military operations center.

(5) Ensures the medical requirements within the detention facility are met consistent with DODI 2310.08E, *Medical Program Support for Detainee Operations,* and its implementing orders and programs. Such requirements will include:

(a) Examining and documenting detainees' physical condition upon initiation of detention.

(b) Monthly recording of detainees' weight.

(c) Monitoring of general cleanliness of the facility (latrines, showers, and wash stations).

(d) Examining detainees for contagious diseases.

(e) Providing detainees access to medical care, such as sick call.

(6) Coordinates for preventive medicine inspections of the facility.

(7) Coordinates preventive medicine inspection of food sources. Advises the DFC of caloric content and dietary suitability of detainee rations.

(8) Coordinates, upon the death of a detainee, with the Armed Forces Medical Examiner (AFME), who will determine if an autopsy is required. The remains will not be released from US custody without authorization from the AFME and the responsible commander.

(9) Clears detainees medically for questioning and interrogation.

(10) Identifies the process for notifying interrogators of detainee medical limitations.

d. **Behavioral Science Consultant (BSC).** BSCs are mental health professionals who receive specialized training in supporting safe, legal, ethical, and effective detention and interrogation operations. In order to maintain clear ethical boundaries, BSCs do not function as health care providers for detainees while engaged in support of interrogation or detainee operations. BSCs normally:

(1) Report directly to the JFC.

(2) Evaluate the psychological strengths and vulnerabilities of detainees, and assist in integrating these factors into a successful interrogation/debriefing process.

(3) Act as consultants to advise detention facility guards, MP, interrogators, military intelligence (MI) personnel, and the command on aspects of the operational environment that will assist in all interrogation and detention operations.

(4) Provide psychological assessments of individual detainees.

(5) Are available to provide mental health support to US personnel involved in detainee operations.

(6) Access directly, consult with, and advise all personnel involved in detention facility operations, intelligence interrogations, and detainee debriefings, including the detention facility chain of command.

e. **Staff Judge Advocate/Legal Advisor**

(1) Serves as the JFC's legal advisor for the CDO.

(2) Advises the commander and other personnel responsible for detainee operations on all matters pertaining to compliance with applicable law and policy.

(3) Provides legal advice to the commander on all matters relating to detainee misconduct.

(4) Advises the appropriate commander regarding investigation of suspected maltreatment or abuse of detainees, or other violations of applicable law or policy.

(5) Serves as the CDO's liaison to the ICRC.

(6) Advises, in coordination with the JFS, the JFC on legal issues pertaining to detainee medical support.

(7) Reviews interrogation plans that use the separation approach and any other plan as directed. Interrogation legal advisors require specialized preparation in interrogation operations to provide consistent, informed advice. A JDIC should have a dedicated counsel.

(8) Advises appropriate commanders on evidentiary collection procedures necessary to prosecute detainees locally for criminal offenses.

(9) Assists with the approval of MISO/information operations (IO) programs as required.

f. **Chaplain**

(1) Serves as the chaplain for the detention facility personnel.

(2) Advises JFC on the religious needs and practices of detainees.

(3) Serves as a moral and ethical advisor for the DFC.

g. **Engineer**

(1) Responsible for the construction, maintenance, and repair of utilities (fire protection, water, electricity, climate control, and sanitation) and upkeep of the detention facility.

(2) Responsible for construction support and ongoing maintenance throughout the lifespan of the facility.

(3) Responsible for construction of force protection measures.

h. **IO Officer**

(1) Develops a comprehensive IO program designed to influence detainees to support current operations.

(2) Coordinates support of information-related capabilities (IRCs) that support detainee-related programs.

(3) Coordinates with the detainee operations lead to represent IRC requirements at the IO working group in support of the commander's intent for detainee operations.

(4) Works with appropriate Joint Staff office of primary responsibility, through the CCDR chain of command, to ensure that transition and reintegration of detainees efforts are supported by IRCs as appropriate.

i. **Public Affairs Officer**

(1) Develops media policies regarding detainee operations for the JFC IAW applicable US law and regulations.

(2) Coordinates all media activity regarding detainees through chain of command.

(3) Coordinates and deconflicts any messages with IO officer.

(4) Reviews detention facility operations from a public affairs perspective and advises the JFC on potential media/public interest.

(5) Responds to media using key command messages consistent with higher public affairs guidance.

(6) Coordinates media visits to theater detention facilities (TDFs).

(7) Works closely with host nation government ministries and agencies and assists them in answering media queries regarding detainee status.

(8) Works closely with the media operations center director.

(9) Monitors media outlets for reporting trends on detainee operations.

(10) Forwards commanders' critical information requirement events of possible national or international media interest to the commander and staff.

(11) Prepares command information products.

(12) Maintains social media sites.

j. **Inspector General**

(1) Reviews detainee operations for all theater sites.

(2) Assists the commander in ensuring adherence to applicable law and policy for detention facility construction and resourcing for logistics.

10. Interagency Representatives

a. Coordinate all visits with the CDO.

b. Coordinate with the DFC and the JIDC commander prior to participation in any interview/interrogation.

11. Multinational Force and Host Nation Representatives

a. Coordinate all visits with the CDO.

b. Coordinate all visits with the DFC for inspections of conditions for detainees captured by their forces.

c. Coordinate with the DFC prior to participation in any interview/interrogation.

Intentionally Blank

CHAPTER III
PLANNING AND CONDUCT OF DETAINEE OPERATIONS

> *"These times of increasing terror[ism] challenge the world. Terror[ism] organizations challenge our comfort and our principles. The United States will continue to take seriously the need to question terrorists who have information that can save lives. But we will not compromise the rule of law or the values and principles that make us strong."*
>
> **President George W. Bush**
> **President's Statement on the United Nations**
> **International Day in Support of Victims of Torture**
> **26 June 2004**

1. Introduction

a. The JFC should consider a plan for detainee operations within the JOA early in the planning cycle of any operation. Planning for detainee operations should be in place prior to the start of operations. The commander should analyze the wide array of logistical and operational requirements to conduct detainee operations. These requirements begin with the correct number and type of personnel on the ground to conduct the operation. Other requirements are the identification, collection, and execution of a logistical plan to support detainee operations throughout the JOA. Plans should adequately account for a potentially very large influx of detainees during the first days of combat operations.

b. The JFC establishes the command and control (C2) relationships among all elements involved in detainee transfers and/or release operations. C2 relationships should be delineated clearly and succinctly (see Figure III-1). C2 guidance, both internal and external to the joint force, should be established as early as possible.

2. Detainee Operations Planning Considerations

JFCs and their staffs should be aware of special planning considerations that history has proven are essential to successful detainee operations. JFCs should anticipate operational and logistical requirements well in advance of conducting detainee operations. Site selection for a detainee facility is critical and must incorporate a wide range of factors including logistical supportability, security, mitigation of escape attempts, and engineering aspects. Consideration should be given to the garrison support activities that support an operating base where detention facilities are located. Comprehensive planning will effectively identify for the DFC and JIDC commander the resources needed to perform all associated garrison support activities that are inherent with facilities of this type. This planning will alleviate potential distractions from the primary mission of detainee operations. See Figure III-2.

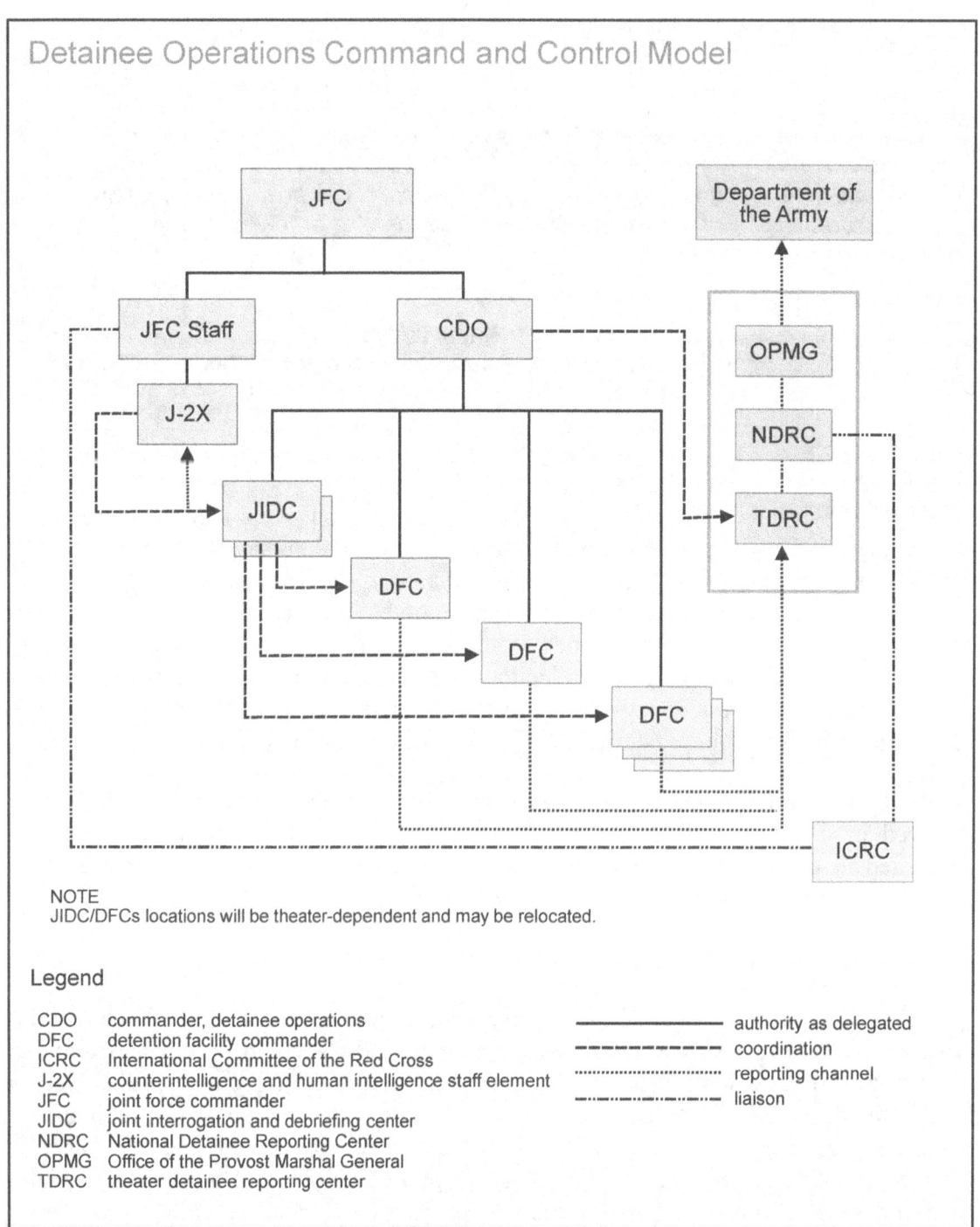

Figure III-1. Detainee Operations Command and Control Model

Examples of Detainee Operations Planning Considerations

- Facility construction materials
- Sanitation requirements
- Medical and dental
- Joint interrogation and debriefing center
- National Detainee Reporting Center communications capability
- Security requirements
- Transportation
- Public affairs
- Legal
- Biometric identification
- Site selection for detention facilities
- Size required for detention facilities
- Garrison support activities

Figure III-2. Examples of Detainee Operations Planning Considerations

3. Other Considerations

As with any operation, proper planning will set the conditions for the successful conduct of detainee operations. To this end, commanders should establish planning mechanisms that ensure effective consideration of potential detainee-related issues and the development of plans and procedures to respond to these issues as early in the planning process as is feasible. Because detainee operations may impact operations, intelligence, logistics, personnel services (human resources support, religious ministry support, financial management, manpower, and legal support), and information aspects of the mission, the detention operations plan requires coordination with all members of the staff. Underestimating the potential number of detainees, especially during initial military operations, has been a planning error in recent conflicts.

a. **Force Protection.** To the maximum extent possible, detainees and places of detention will be protected from the hazards of the battlefield. Detainees should derive the same benefit from force protection measures as do members of the detaining force.

b. **Logistics.** Logistics considerations should be reflected in the time-phased force and deployment data. The following issues are a few examples of some of the unique logistic obligations and considerations associated with detention operations:

(1) **Temperature and Lighting.** To the extent feasible, the facilities will be protected from dampness, adequately heated and cooled, and appropriately illuminated.

(2) **Food and Water.** When feasible, detainees will be fed three meals a day. At a minimum, basic daily food rations will be sufficient in quantity, quality, and variety to keep detainees in good health and to prevent significant weight loss or development of nutritional deficiencies. The justification for any deviation from the three meals per day standard will be documented by the commander of the detention facility and should be reviewed by both medical and legal support personnel. The habitual diet and religious/cultural requirements of the detainees will be taken into account. The detaining power will supply detainees who work with such additional rations as are necessary for the labor in which they are employed. Sufficient water for drinking and hygiene will be supplied to detainees.

(3) **Clothing.** Adequate clothing for the climate will be provided, and a clothing replacement program will be instituted at each facility. Issued clothing should be uniform in color for identification purposes. If replacement clothing is not available, commanders will attempt to provide for the cleaning of detainee clothing in order to protect the health and well-being of detainees until a clothing exchange program can be instituted.

(4) **Financial Management.** The JFC is responsible for providing EPWs and CIs pay. The joint task force comptroller may designate a component to provide currency and other required support. The designated component will also ensure that controls are established to process deposits to and payments from designated accounts properly. Refer to Defense Finance and Accounting Service–Indianapolis Regulation 37-1, *Finance and Accounting Policy Implementation,* Chapter 26, for specific information pertaining to detainee pay.

(5) **Medical Care, Dental Care, and Sanitation.** The detaining power will take all sanitary measures necessary to ensure the cleanliness and healthfulness of facilities, and to prevent epidemics. Detainees will have access to sanitary facilities that conform to preventive medicine sanitation standards. In facilities where women detainees are accommodated, feminine hygiene supplies will be provided. Detainees will receive a full medical history and physical exam during in-processing. A medical record will be created for each detainee, and a narrative summary of that record will be forwarded to the detainee's new facility location. If the detainee is released, he/she should be given a narrative clinical summary detailing past and present medical status and recommendation of medical follow-up, if any. All treatment provider names will be redacted. No records will be released directly to the detainee or a foreign country. Patient services should include first responder, forward resuscitative, and theater hospitalization capabilities, as operational circumstances permit. As a contribution to the maintenance of good order, the DFCs should also provide mental health services (mental health treatment, assessment, and therapy) to detainees when feasible.

(6) **Work Program.** The JFC establishes appropriate policy and guidelines for the detainee work programs, to include validation of the funding requirement through the appropriate resourcing channels within theater.

c. **Property Safekeeping and Confiscation Accountability.** DODD 2310.01E, *Department of Defense Detainee Program,* states, "Detainees and their property shall be accounted for and records maintained according to applicable law, regulation, policy or other issuances." All personal effects and articles of personal use (except arms, military equipment, personal documents with intelligence value, and military documents) will remain in the possession of detainees, including effects and articles used for their clothing or feeding, unless the detaining force considers continued possession to cause a risk for the detaining force or other detainees, or the item is of intelligence or law enforcement value. Detainees will be permitted to retain individual protective gear and like articles issued for personal protection. This is especially important during initial detention and transportation to a more established detention facility when there is a risk that the detainees will be exposed to chemical, biological, radiological, and nuclear threats. This rule does not prohibit the centralized management of such protective equipment by the DFC if such management is intended to enhance the overall protection of detainees. Badges of rank and nationality, decorations, and articles having, above all, a personal or sentimental value, may not be taken from detainees. Sums of money carried by detainees may not be taken away from them except by order of a commanding officer, after the amount and particulars of the owner have been recorded in a special register, and an itemized receipt has been given, legibly inscribed with the name, rank, and unit of the person issuing the said receipt. Sums in the currency of the detaining power, or those changed into such currency at the detainee's request, will be placed to the credit of the detainee's account. The detaining power may temporarily confiscate articles of value or necessity, including medications, from detainees when such action is determined to be necessary for reasons of security (including intelligence evaluations for the purpose of the security of the force). Procedures for such confiscation should be established by SOP and should follow the rules applicable for the impoundment of money noted above. All personal property taken from detainees shall be kept in the custody of the detaining power and, if feasible, shall be returned in its initial condition to the detainees at the end of their detention. Always use a chain of custody receipt for inventoried numbers. Administrative detainee property practices may not be adequate to preserve evidence. If detainee property is needed as evidence in criminal proceedings, military law rules of evidence should be followed.

d. **Administrative Processing and Accountability.** According to DODD 2310.01E, *Department of Defense Detainee Program,* DOD components shall maintain full accountability for all detainees under DOD control. Detainee records and reports shall be maintained, safeguarded, and provided to the Under Secretary of Defense for Policy and other DOD components, as appropriate. Information and biometric samples and associated data will be collected and recorded on each detainee captured and detained by the Armed Forces of the United States and referenced to the ISN. Detainees should provide name, rank, serial number (if applicable), and date of birth for tracking purposes and appropriate country notification. However, failure to do so does not result in any treatment not otherwise consistent with this publication. Upon transfer to a theater-level facility, detainee information (including information related to personal property taken from the detainee) will be provided to the National Detainee Reporting Center (NDRC) through the TDRC. The NDRC will maintain all information concerning detainees and their property.

e. **Religious, Intellectual, and Physical Activities**

(1) **Religion.** Respect for the religious preferences of detainees is an essential aspect of detainee operations. Accordingly, the organization and administration of the

detention facility must not be such as to hinder unjustifiably the observance of religious rites, and commanders should plan for the reasonable accommodation of the religious needs of detainees. Certain limitations may be necessary due to security concerns. However, a good faith balance should be struck between the detainee's obligation to comply with disciplinary rules and procedures and the detaining power's obligation to afford detainees the ability to meet their religious obligations and exercise their religious practices. The detaining power is also prohibited from imposing any adverse distinctions within the detainee population based on religion. In this regard, it should be noted that in some situations, segregating the detainee population based on religious affiliation may be beneficial and therefore not prohibited, particularly when conflict has been based in part on religious affiliation. Detainees have no right to person-to-person support by military chaplains. Therefore JFCs are under no obligation to provide such support. Accordingly, military chaplains do not generally provide direct religious support to detainees. Should the JFC determine a requirement to provide direct military chaplain support to detainees, communications between the chaplains and the detainees will be privileged to the extent provided by Military Rule of Evidence 503 and appropriate Military Department policies.

(2) **Physical and Intellectual Activities.** Physical and intellectual activities for detainees contribute to the maintenance of good order and discipline within the detainee population. Commanders may accommodate these interests when doing so is both feasible and consistent with mission requirements. The extent to which accommodation is considered and/or implemented will be determined by the needs of the facility population and will take into account both security limitations and available resources. Authorized activities and programs include, but are not limited to, participation in physical exercise, access to outdoor areas, and the practice of intellectual, educational, and recreational pursuits. Other programs that may be considered, where feasible and consistent with security limitations and/or mission accomplishment, include establishment of a family visitation program.

(3) Detainees should have voluntary access to a wide array of programs. These programs help protect moderate detainees from extremist influence, prepare detainees for release, and encourage them to not engage in belligerent activities when released. While the programs must be tailored for each area and conflict, they can include vocational, educational (especially reading and writing), and religious programs.

f. **The ICRC and NGOs and Other Similar Organizations**

(1) During detainee operations, commanders may encounter representatives of organizations attempting to protect detainee interests. Such representatives will often seek access to detainees, and/or offer their services to assist in the care and maintenance of detainees. Effective detainee operations planning will establish a mechanism for command interaction with such organizations in order to maximize the benefit of potential contributions to the US effort. Commanders should anticipate that, upon initiation of detainee operations, these organizations will request access to and/or information about detainees, and they will continue to do so throughout the operation. Commanders should seek guidance through operational command channels for responding to such requests prior to the initiation of detainee operations, or as soon thereafter as possible. In the absence of

mission-specific guidance, all such requests for access or information should flow via the established chain of command to the Office of the Secretary of Defense (OSD).

(2) The ICRC is an independent, neutral organization ensuring humanitarian protection and assistance for victims of war and armed violence. The ICRC has a permanent mandate under international law to take impartial action for prisoners, the wounded and sick, and civilians affected by conflict. The Geneva Conventions give it a unique status. Commanders should be cognizant of the special status of the ICRC. Per DOD policy, the ICRC is the only organization presumptively authorized access to detainees. Consistent with the Geneva Conventions, it is DOD policy that the ICRC shall be allowed to offer its services during an armed conflict, however characterized, to which the US is a party. ICRC access to detainees is subject to temporary suspension based on imperative considerations of military necessity. As a general rule, commanders should coordinate with a legal and public affairs advisor before ordering a suspension of ICRC access to a detainee.

g. **Media.** Detainees will be protected from public curiosity at all times. Strict compliance with this requirement is essential. There is no distinction between international and domestic media with regard to this obligation. Media attention concerning detainees is likely to be substantial. Commanders and staffs should anticipate such attention and ensure that supporting public affairs personnel develop procedures, in advance, for dealing with media requests for visits and information. Unless delegated to subordinate commanders, OSD is the sole release authority for photographs or video of detainees. Commanders will prepare and coordinate, in advance, public affairs plans for events such as detainee movements, transfers, or releases, with both the transferring and receiving commanders.

(1) Requests for interviews or filming of detainees must be coordinated through the staff judge advocate to ensure compliance with applicable laws and regulations including the law of war.

(2) Photographing, filming, or other videotaping of detainees for other than internal detention facility management and intelligence purposes is prohibited.

(3) Individuals in the custody or under the physical control of the USG, regardless of nationality or physical location, shall not be subjected to cruel, inhumane, or degrading treatment or punishment.

4. Internment Serial Number

a. IAW DODD 2310.01E, *Department of Defense Detainee Program,* individuals who are retained by DOD personnel shall be vetted and assigned an ISN as soon as possible. The ISN is the DOD identification number used to maintain accountability of detainees. (See Figure III-3.) All detainees under DOD control will be registered promptly, normally within 14 days of capture. Once an ISN is assigned, all further documentation, including medical records, will use only this number (no other numbering system will be used). The ISN is generated by the detainee reporting system (DRS), the detainee accountability database required for use by all DOD agencies. The ISN is comprised of five components:

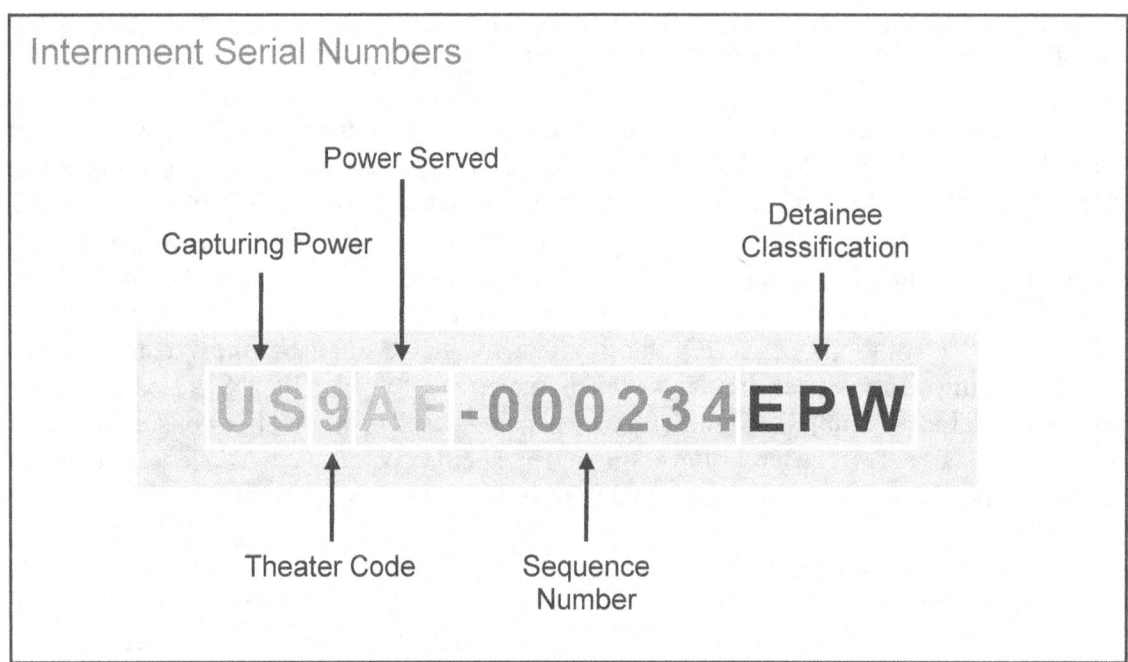

Figure III-3. Internment Serial Numbers

(1) *First Component.* The two-digit alpha character code representing the capturing power. Only country codes found within the Defense Human Intelligence Enterprise-Manual (DHE-M) 3301.001, *Defense Human Intelligence (HUMINT) Enterprise-Manual, Volume I: Collection Requirements, Reporting, and Evaluation Procedures,* or its successor, will be used.

(2) *Second Component.* The single-digit designation of the command/theater under which the detainee came into the custody of the US.

(3) *Third Component.* The two-digit alpha character code representing the detainee's power served/nationality. Where applicable, country codes found within DHE-M 3301.001, *Defense Human Intelligence (HUMINT) Enterprise-Manual, Volume I: Collection Requirements, Reporting, and Evaluation Procedures,* or its successor, will be used.

(4) *Fourth Component.* A unique six-digit number assigned exclusively to an individual detainee. The DRS will assign these numbers sequentially. This component is commonly referred to as the "sequence number." Not even in the event of a detainee's death, release, repatriation, transfer, or escape, will a sequence number be reissued during the course of a single conflict to another detainee. If a detainee is ever issued two sequence numbers, the later number will be voided and the NDRC will be notified.

(5) *Fifth Component.* A two- or three-digit alpha character code representing the detainee's classification. The ISN, once issued, is reported through the TDRC to the NDRC. Once the DRS has created an ISN, no component may be changed or corrected at the theater level without approval from the NDRC. All changes to an ISN must be requested in writing and approved by the NDRC.

> **Operation ENDURING FREEDOM country codes are found within the superseded Defense Intelligence Agency Manual 58-12, Appendix A.**

b. When required by law and/or policy, the NDRC provides detainee information to the ICRC to satisfy Geneva Convention obligations. The ICRC uses this information to provide notice of the status of the detained individual to his or her government. The US must be vigilant in executing all obligations to account for detainees and must issue detainees an ISN when required by law and/or policy. Commanders should make every effort to standardize tracking detainees from point of capture through the issuance of an ISN. The unique capture tag number that is found on Department of Defense Form (DD) 2745, *Enemy Prisoner of War (EPW) Capture Tag,* or allied equivalent, is the only authorized tracking number that may be used prior to the assignment of an ISN. After the ISN is assigned, previously generated documents should be annotated with the ISN. For example, medical personnel should use the capture tag number and then use an ISN, once an ISN is issued to a detainee, to track a detainee through the medical treatment facilities and back to the detention facility. Biometric samples should be labeled with the detainee's ISN when being submitted to a laboratory or authoritative database for processing, and associated data annotated accordingly when being stored or transmitted. The DRS cross references the ISN and the capture tag number for administrative purposes.

c. IAW National Security Presidential Directive 59/Homeland Security Presidential Directive 24, *Biometrics for Identification and Screening to Enhance National Security,* all individuals detained during military operations and assigned an ISN for engaging in conduct constituting, preparing for, aiding, or relating to enemy acts against US, allied, and/or multinational forces, excluding any individual detained solely as an EPW, shall be categorized as potential threats to national security. Based on this designation, biometric and biographic information on these individuals will be made available to front-line screening organizations to support future privilege or access decisions. Complete and accurate collections of biometric, biographic, contextual, and derogatory information on detainees upon intake and throughout the period of DOD control is critical to support future operational decisions at the point of encounter. Similarly, based upon information, events, and materials associated with the captured individual, many detainees may meet the criteria for nomination to the National Known or Suspected Terrorist Watch List. This watch list is used by front-line screening organizations to control entry into the United States or its territories, as well as the sovereign boundaries of many of our allies, and in some cases access to major transportation systems (air, rail, etc.). Complete and accurate information collected at the point of capture, especially during early periods of conflict when the rate of detention may be at its highest, is critical. Sometimes, it is solely the information recorded on the DD 2745, *Enemy Prisoner of War (EPW) Capture Tag,* that facilitates an accepted known or suspected terrorist watch list nomination.

5. **Detainee Control and Discipline**

Maintaining control and discipline within a detention facility is essential to detainee operations. JFCs will ensure that DFCs establish procedures for detainee control and discipline. Because imposition of corporal punishment is inconsistent with the humane treatment obligation, commanders must understand the relationship between reward and punishment. As a general rule, withdrawal of privileges provided above the minimum required level of humane treatment is often the most effective sanction for disciplinary infractions, and granting additional privileges is often the most effective incentive for continued compliance and cooperation. Planning for the provision of such privileges is therefore an essential component to any discipline and control program. Other considerations for maintaining control and discipline include, but are not limited to:

a. SOPs regarding positive control measures over detainees, including use of biometrics systems to verify detainee identities at locations throughout the facility.

b. Procedures to ensure detainees understand rules, regulations, and expectations of compliance. Those rules and regulations shall be posted for detainees in their native language.

c. Viable mechanisms for detainees to raise grievances to the chain of command.

d. Privilege-granting and withdrawal processes to enhance compliance.

e. SOP regarding physical compliance measures when lesser means have been or would be ineffective. For more information, see Appendix C, "Detention Facility Riot Control Measures."

f. Prohibition of fraternization between detainees and detention facility personnel.

g. SOPs regarding prevention of escape attempts.

h. A rewards and penalty program. For those detainees who are uncooperative and high risk, the Geneva Conventions address the minimal level of treatment and entitlements.

6. Training Standards and Documentation for Detainee Operations

The Office of the Provost Marshal General has primary Headquarters, Department of the Army responsibility for the DOD Detainee Programs. When US forces conduct detainee operations, they must possess the text of the applicable Geneva Conventions and be instructed as to their provisions. JFCs have the overall responsibility to develop, implement, monitor, and, when necessary, refine standards, policies, and SOPs for detainee operations that are consistent with obligations imposed by law and applicable policy. Pursuant to this obligation, JFCs are responsible to ensure the effective routine review of detainee operations and related training to enhance compliance with applicable law and policy. All guard force commands and respective attachments will establish a continuous training program; training regularly on emergency plans, to include disturbance control formations, use of force, first aid, interpersonal communication skill training, and nonlethal munitions usage. DFCs will maintain records of all relevant documents regarding the conduct of detainee operations. These records will be available for review during all inspections and assessments of the detainee operation.

CHAPTER IV
CAPTURE AND INITIAL DETENTION AND SCREENING OF DETAINEES

> *"Humane Treatment. The requirement that protected persons must at all times be humanely treated is the basic theme of the Geneva Conventions."*
>
> **Jean S. Pictet's Commentary to the Geneva Convention Relative to the Treatment of Prisoners of War, Article 13, 1958**

1. Introduction

a. In any given JOA, any element of the joint force may find itself on a mission in which individuals are captured or placed under the control of US forces. The efficient and effective control, processing, detention, and intelligence exploitation of such personnel is often critical to the success of US forces. The humane treatment and proper care of detained personnel support US mission success.

b. Capture or detention may occur during any military operation. Commanders, their staffs, and subordinate forces must anticipate this reality, and plan and train accordingly.

2. Capture and Initial Screening

a. Once the capture of individuals has occurred, the proper identification and classification of those personnel is critical to the overall intelligence and detainee operations effort. Rapid collection of biometrics information from detainees is critical to ensuring their prompt identification, and is a crucial step that must be conducted as soon as possible after detention. The initial classification of a detainee may be based on unsupported statements or documentation accompanying the detainee. After a detainee is assigned to a facility, expect a continuing need for further classification. If the identity of the detainee was based on unsupported statements or documentation, the detainee may be reclassified as more information is obtained. Tactical commanders must exercise discretion when determining whether an individual poses a credible threat or possesses sufficient information requiring evacuation and detention. All joint force components will establish collection points that meet established standards within their specific operational area.

b. Individuals captured or detained by US forces must be evacuated expeditiously through transit points to reach a detention facility in a secure area. Capturing units should have supplies of the following equipment: flex-cuffs, blackened goggles, zip-lock bags, trash bags, duct tape, DD 2745, *Enemy Prisoner of War (EPW) Capture Tag,* and evidence/property custody documents. When captured, detainees will normally be held at the DCP pending their evacuation. The DCP will support the rapid transfer of control from capturing forces to US MP or other approved units for custody and control. Capturing units may conduct tactical questioning for combat information relative to the commander's critical information requirements IAW DODD 3115.09, *DOD Intelligence Interrogations, Detainee Debriefings, and Tactical Questioning,* and DOD approved policies. DOD personnel who conduct, support, or participate in tactical questioning shall be trained, at a minimum, in the law of war and humane treatment standards. The detainee guard force at DCP facilities should have supplies of the following equipment: biometrics collection devices, restraints, latex examination gloves, flex-cuffs, civil disturbance gear, and nonlethal weapons. The DCP should be located close to the area of actual operations for quick detainee evacuation, but also be situated in a safe, secure location for both detainees and the security force. Appropriate segregation of detainees will be implemented as early as feasible in the detention process. While at the detention facility, a determination must be made regarding further evacuation for strategic intelligence exploitation and dissemination. It should therefore be located close to the area of actual operations for quick evacuation of detainees, but should also be situated in a location intended to provide for the safety and security of the detainees and the security force. For example, the DCP could normally be located in a brigade support area of the brigade combat team, or an equivalent type unit. Detainees should be transported from the DCP to the detainee holding area (DHA) as soon as practicable. The DHA will normally be located in a secure location that provides safety and is easily accessible for receipt and evacuation of detainees. Upon arrival at the DHA, HUMINT collectors will normally screen all arriving detainees to determine those suspected of possessing information of immediate tactical value. The DCP will coordinate with the supporting higher headquarters for the evacuation of detainees using organic assets to the DHA. Detainee status determinations will not be made at the DHA. IAW DOD policy, all detainees will be treated humanely at all times and locations.

c. The DHA should be located in a secure area with easy access to transportation nodes, but must be protected from the effects of the battlefield to the extent feasible. To the extent possible, accommodation must be made for female and child detainees. Unless militarily infeasible, female detainees must be searched by female service members and must be segregated from male detainees. If possible, increased numbers of HUMINT collectors should be available for exploitation activities at the DHA.

d. Detainees will be transported to a TDF based on intelligence exploitation and transportation availability, at which point they will normally be assigned an ISN. All detainees will be in-processed and receive an ISN immediately upon arrival. Additionally, biometric collection is mandatory during detainee in-processing. An MP detention battalion, with the appropriate units assigned, will conduct operations at a TDF with a specific capacity of up to 4,000 detainees, based on a docile, compliant population. Units will mark and tag all detainee-associated documents and property and transfer the documents and property to the transporting unit for movement to the TDF. This will maintain detainee property accountability and provide for further analysis and evaluation by DOD-trained HUMINT collectors and/or certified interrogators.

e. Detainees will not be accepted for detainment or transfer to US military control from other nations without prior approval from OSD. The officer designated to accept them will properly account for all detainees received. The receipt (DD 2708, Receipt for Inmate or Detained Person) indicates the place and date the facility assumed custody and the name, grade, and nationality of each transferred detainee.

f. Prior planning, close coordination, and synchronization of assets with all resources used for the transportation of detainees to the TDF are required. Planning considerations should include proximity to DCPs and TDFs within the JOA, transportation responsibilities (air, land, and sea), logistic support (for real-time and future operations), and medical support for all DHAs and TDFs within the JOA. A TDF is an improved, semipermanent, or permanent facility that can hold detainees until they are released or until it is determined that out-of-theater evacuation is necessary. JFCs should carefully evaluate the need to establish and maintain more than one TDF in a JOA. Associated costs, manning requirements, and logistic sustainability may not allow for operating more than one TDF. Ideally, the TDF will have:

(1) Sufficient MP and corrections specialists once the theater has matured.

(2) Permanent structures, lighting, water, utilities, and hygiene and sanitation facilities.

(3) Ability to provide forward resuscitation, theater hospitalization, and higher medical care to detainees.

(4) Religious and morale facilities.

(5) Networked information system for issuing ISNs and maintaining the detainee database in the DRS.

(6) Communications capability (for accountability of detainees through to the TDRC/NDRC).

(7) Support for all classes of supply and services.

g. An interview area should be established near the TDF receiving/processing line so that intelligence personnel can interview detainees and examine their equipment and documents after they have been assigned an ISN. If detainees or their equipment or documents are removed from the receiving/processing line, accountability must be maintained IAW applicable SOPs.

h. If a detainee's status is in doubt in an international armed conflict, a tribunal will be conducted IAW Article 5, GPW. The protections afforded EPWs under the GPW will apply to such individuals until their status is determined.

i. Certified HUMINT and counterintelligence personnel will conduct further exploitation at the TDF. In addition to responding to the commander's critical information requirements and validated intelligence collection requirements, they support the detainee disposition process by providing recommendations to release, continue to hold, or transport the detainee to the strategic detention facility. Trained organic MP personnel can identify individuals with potential to provide significant force protection information that may assist the DFC in maintaining security and good order in the detainee population. However, MP personnel are prohibited from actively participating in intelligence interrogations.

j. Employing MP as far forward as possible will assist the tactical maneuver commanders by freeing up combat assets to accomplish their missions.

k. The NDRC serves as the national collection center for detainee information. The TDRC is assigned to the MP brigade and functions as the field operations agency for the NDRC. It is the central agency responsible for maintaining and reporting information on all detainees and their personal property within an assigned theater. The CDO reports detainee accountability of persons and property of their facility/facilities to the TDRC every 24 hours via Department of the Army Form 2674-R-E, *Enemy Prisoner of War/Civilian Internee Strength Report (LRA)*, which is submitted through the DRS. The TDRC reviews and reports detainee accountability of persons and property within an assigned theater to the NDRC every 24 hours via Department of the Army Form 2674-R-E, *Enemy Prisoner of War/Civilian Internee Strength Report (LRA)*, which is submitted through the DRS. These reports are critical to ensure continued compliance with applicable US law, the law of war, and DOD policy. Note: MP detention battalions may report directly to NDRC when a TDRC is not operating in theater.

3. **Secondary Screening and Confirmation**

The tactical commander/leader has responsibilities to properly handle and prepare detainees for subsequent transfer to a DHA or TDF. Additionally, DFCs and interrogation commanders must have clearly defined secondary screening and confirmation policies and procedures to receive detainees from point of capture units. Commanders at each level should ensure the following steps are taken when handling detainees.

a. **Point of Capture Units.** Units below battalion will be trained on how to conduct tactical questioning and make recommendations to MI personnel on potential detainees of intelligence value. Detainee capture kits need to be issued to capturing units to assist in the proper identification, securing, and transporting of detainees. These kits may include biometrics collection devices, buccal swabs for DNA ([deoxyribonucleic acid] collection), latex gloves, surgical masks, flex-cuffs, earmuffs, capture tags, and property bags along with property custody documents. Each detainee must arrive at the DHA or TDF with a completed capture tag and the required information that can be found in the detainee tagging kit. JFCs may implement additional measures beyond the required capture tag. Proper completion of the capture tag is important to intelligence collection, detainee status determination, and the decision to retain or release. Failure to provide a properly annotated capture tag may substantially degrade the ability to process the detainee effectively, and it may result in the denial of acceptance of detainees at a facility until the required paperwork is completed and turned over to the new facility.

b. **Daily Detainee Operations.** DFCs will establish policies and procedures for the detention and interrogation of detainees in the detention facility. Such policies must be consistent with applicable US law and policy. All locations where detainees are held by US forces will, to the extent feasible, be shielded from the dangers associated with military operations. Commanders should attempt to utilize building-type structures for internment facilities. However, although this may be a preference, there is no prohibition against using less-improved facilities when they offer the best available option for satisfying all legal and policy obligations related to detainee treatment. There is no legal requirement to provide detainees with conditions better than those of the US forces executing the detainee operation mission.

(1) It is important, either at the DHA or the TDF, that certified HUMINT and counterintelligence personnel have access to the detainees as quickly as possible. An interview site will be established near the receiving/processing line so that MI personnel can screen detainees and examine their equipment and documents. This will either facilitate the release of those who do not meet holding criteria or expedite exploitation of relevant and timely information in support of the intelligence process.

(2) Another critical aspect of detainee operations is record-keeping utilizing a common database that can be used by all personnel coming in contact with each detainee. As detainees are in-processed, a medical screening will be conducted during which the height and weight of each detainee are recorded. In addition, any marks or injuries on the detainees will be annotated and recorded. Commanders should also consider including medical screening to include any medication that could affect the credibility of the information provided prior to and subsequent to interrogations. A daily log will be maintained on each detainee and will include, at a minimum, records of any injuries, times of interrogations, times of medical exams, any hunger strikes and their durations, as well as any disciplinary problems and corrective measures taken. This information will be provided to the next detention facility if a detainee is transferred.

(3) Detainees will be segregated within detention facilities according to the distinctions specified by law and policy, unless such segregation is not possible due to the conditions of the facility. If the TDF commander determines that such segregation is required by law, but the facility's conditions prevent segregation, the commander will attempt to develop other methods of protecting the interests of detainees, and will request the additional resources required to provide for such segregation.

(4) The guard force will become familiar with simple commands to be given in the language of the detainee population. Detention facilities will provide and post copies of the applicable Geneva Conventions for detainees in their own language.

c. **Detainee Death**

(1) If a detainee in US custody dies, the commander, the staff judge advocate or legal adviser, and appropriate military investigative agency will be notified immediately. The attending medical officer will provide the commander the following information:

      (a) Full name of deceased.

      (b) ISN of deceased.

      (c) Date and place of death.

      (d) A statement as to the cause of death.

Military police (MP) or authorized guard force personnel will escort the detainee to the joint interrogation and debriefing center (JIDC), which is located in close proximity to the detention facility. Depending on local standard operating procedures, security concerns, and force manning levels, the human intelligence (HUMINT) collectors and certified interrogators may request that escorts remain to guard the detainee, or they may release the escorts until the detainee needs to be returned to the living area. Release of custody must be officially documented. The JIDC personnel will never use locally contrived aliases or false names on detainee records. A six-digit field reporter number (FRN) may be substituted for the collector's name on chain of custody receipts. (An FRN should be requested through the command counterintelligence and HUMINT staff element to the Defense Intelligence Agency.) The only authorized purpose for escorts to remain in the HUMINT collection area is to provide for custody and control of the detainee. MP or other security personnel will not be involved in the interrogation process or set conditions for interrogations.

(2) After coordination with the AFME, the detention facility's senior medical officer available will sign the death certificate. This authority will not be delegated. Upon the death of a detainee, the detention facility, unit, or medical facility will immediately notify the TDRC through the chain of command by the most expeditious means possible.

(3) The DFC will initiate a serious incident report.

(4) As soon as possible, with permission from the responsible military investigative agency, biometrically confirm the identity of the deceased detainee.

d. **JIDC.** A JIDC is located in close proximity to a TDF. The DFC and the intelligence operations commander will develop procedures that include accountability and security responsibilities for detainees when they are undergoing interrogation. HUMINT collectors will coordinate with the TDF commander in order to obtain detainee information gathered by organic MP personnel through passive custodial observation and conversation.

4. Transfers

a. "Transfers" refers to the movement of detainees between DOD locations. Typically a transfer will also change the officer responsible for the detainee's accountability and well-being.

b. During the course of their detention, detainees may be transferred between relatively local TDFs, across international borders, or to other suitable locations outside the combat zone. Orders directing detainee transfers usually will include detailed coordinating instructions regarding the method of transportation. Movement may involve multiple modes of transportation and coordination between the Services to effect the transfer.

> "The Detaining Power shall take adequate precautions especially in case of transport by sea or by air, to ensure their safety during transfer, and shall draw up a complete list of all transferred prisoners before their departure."
>
> **Excerpt from Article 46, Geneva Convention**
> **Relative to the Treatment of Prisoners of War**

c. Security and safety are principal concerns when planning a transfer. Security must include safeguards for US and multinational force personnel, government property, and the detainees. Further considerations include contingency plans for and prevention of escape attempts, attacks upon the detainee movement, delays en route due to enemy actions, weather, and mechanical failures.

d. Plans must include provisions for adequate food, water, and shelter. The movement should not expose the detainees to undue hazards. Consideration for individual detainee needs (e.g., adequate supplies of prescription medication, medical support en route, and sanitary and hygienic needs) must also be addressed.

e. Extended trips may require guard force rotation and rest plans.

5. Detainee Movement Planning

The primary considerations for detainee escort missions are the security of the conveyance, the safety of all US resources, and the protection of the detainees. The coordination for the transportation of detainees is the responsibility of the detaining power and is a task that must be performed by military personnel. The foremost planning consideration is assessing the appropriate amount of land, maritime, and air transportation assets to accomplish the mission. Considerations will also be made for the logistical, medical, and linguistic needs of detainees while in transit. Given the array of transportation methods and variety of arrangements, no single instruction can feasibly outline all tactics, techniques, and procedures to be used throughout all detainee escort missions. Therefore, it is necessary for commanders, security elements, and other personnel to use their best judgment when selecting a course of action to accomplish this task. Ideally, the issues related to detainee transport should be addressed in orders or directives issued by the JFC.

6. Procedures

a. DFCs will forward copies of detainee records (including at a minimum: capture tag, disciplinary actions, medical narrative summaries, property, and record of any injuries sustained since capture) along with a complete manifest for each detainee transferred. Prior to transport from the DHA to a TDF, all detainees will receive a thorough medical exam, and be deloused, bathed, and, if necessary, shaved. Detainees will be thoroughly searched for weapons and contraband immediately before boarding the conveyance. Detainees will be briefed in a language that they understand about the departure and restrictions while on board the conveyance, as well as safety and emergency procedures. Detainee records and property will accompany them during transport.

b. Another aspect of transfer missions is the transportation of detainees to medical treatment facilities or to judicial proceedings. These transfer missions are likely to involve many security assets—therefore, commanders should conduct a thorough mission analysis and determine appropriate requirements for such transport missions. Therefore, they should be considered when planning detainee operations.

7. Detainee Movement by Land Transportation

JFCs should plan for and assign the mission of detainee evacuation to a properly resourced transportation element. The transportation of detainees is a separate mission from the escort and guarding of detainees in transit. Capturing units and initial transfers will primarily use land transportation. Further movement of detainees by land transportation should be minimized to limit exposure to hazards, public curiosity, and the media.

8. Detainee Movement by Maritime Transportation

Detainee movement by maritime transportation can be used, but normally it will not be considered as a location for detention (in rare circumstances, temporary maritime detention may provide the best course of action to protect detainees from operational and environmental hazards). If considered, the use of maritime detention must be authorized by Secretary of Defense (SecDef). When maritime movement is used, appropriate resources and areas aboard maritime vessels will be sequestered for detainee use and must meet the requirements of the Geneva Conventions. See Appendix B, "Detainee Operations at Sea."

9. Detainee Movement by Air Transportation

Detainee movement by air should be the primary means of transporting detainees outside the JOA. Aircrews that are responsible for the transportation of detainees will be briefed on the proper handling and interacting procedures. Security escort teams will be trained for the mission and perform all detainee handling procedures on board the aircraft. The security escort team leader will adopt tactics, techniques, and procedures to meet mission requirements, including feeding, latrine escort, medical aid, and any emergency actions aboard the conveyance. A copy of the detainee manifest will remain with the losing organization until the detainees are accounted for at the gaining unit.

10. Detainee Disposition

A detainee disposition describes the intended status of a detainee's liberty, confinement, or fate upon release from DOD control. A disposition will be indicated on release or repatriation orders generated by the DRS.

a. **Repatriation**

(1) Is a term applied only to EPW/RP when leaving DOD control for return to their country.

(2) Repatriation or accommodation of sick or wounded EPWs/RP in a neutral country may occur during hostilities.

(3) Sick and wounded prisoners will not be repatriated against their will during hostilities.

(4) EPW/RP who are not repatriated under the above circumstances will be repatriated at the cessation of hostilities as directed by OSD.

(5) EPW/RP eligible for repatriation but WHO have judicial proceedings pending for offenses not exclusively subject to disciplinary punishment will be detained until the close of the proceedings.

b. **Release**

(1) A term applied to all types of detainees, other than EPW/RP, when leaving DOD control. Note that in certain cases, "release" means that the detainee will be transferred to the control of another government or USG department or agency.

(2) Detainees may be released during or after a period of conflict.

(3) Release orders may further specify the reason for a detainee release or declare their intended post-release disposition. The DRS will contain a menu of release options. Common options are:

(a) Detainee Review Board—a detainee has gone through the standard review for release and is approved for a general release from custody, usually on the detainee's own recognizance.

(b) Higher Headquarters Order—theater commander orders the release of a detainee, omitting the requirement for a detainee review board.

(c) Released to Alternate Authority—detainee is released to a partner nation's military.

(d) Released to Country of Origin—detainee is released to the government of the detainee's origin. This selection is used to release third-country nationals to their home nations.

(e) Released to Host Nation—detainee is released to the local equivalent of law enforcement or corrections officers.

(f) Released to Local Civil Authority—a detainee is released to the local equivalent of law enforcement or corrections officers.

(g) Released to NGOs—detainee is released to an organization that has no affiliation to any government, for the purpose of returning the detainees to their home nations. This would include organizations such as the ICRC.

(h) Released to other USG departments or agencies—detainee is released to another US non-DOD entity.

c. **Escape.** Self-explanatory.

d. **Death.** Self-explanatory.

e. **Disposition Responsibilities**

(1) **JFC**

(a) Provide all personnel conducting detainee operations training and logistical support necessary to conduct transfer or release operations.

(b) Develop and conduct all transfer and/or release operations IAW applicable US law and policy.

(c) Determine air, land, or maritime transportation requirements for transfer and/or release operations to the point of capture, through the unit responsible for that JOA.

(d) Establish the C2 relationship between all elements involved in transfer and/or release operations.

(e) Provide notification of the transfer and/or release of a detainee to the NDRC.

(f) Coordinate with appropriate staff elements to conduct transfer or release operations.

(g) Coordinate with appropriate commanders and staffs to ensure that transfer or release operations directives are disseminated throughout the JOA.

(2) **JFS**

(a) Ensure policies established regarding medical requirements for the transfer or release of detainees are IAW applicable US law and policy.

(b) Ensure coordination of subordinate medical elements to support transfer or release operations.

(3) **Staff Judge Advocate**

(a) Provide the JFC with legal guidance regarding applicable US law and regulations.

(b) Serve as the command liaison to the ICRC and advise the command concerning ICRC activities related to the transfer/release of detainees.

(c) Provide technical expertise in support of required instruction and training related to the law of war.

(4) **Public Affairs Officer**

(a) Develop media policies regarding detainee operations for the JFC IAW applicable US law and policy.

(b) Coordinate all media coverage regarding detainee transfer or release operations through the chain of command.

11. Detainee Classification

The initial classification of a detainee may be based on unsupported statements or documentation accompanying the detainee. After a detainee is assigned to a facility, expect a continuing need for further classification. If the identity of the detainee may have been based on unsupported statements or documentation, it may be necessary to reclassify the detainee as more information is obtained. If the detainee's classification remains in doubt, a tribunal may be convened to determine the detainee's status. Reclassification may result in release of detainees, or reassignment of detainees within the facility or to other facilities.

12. Review and Approval Process

a. For transfer or release authority of US-captured detainees, SecDef, or SecDef's designee, will establish criteria for the transfer or release of detainees and communicate those criteria to all commanders operating within the theater.

b. The designated CCDRs will periodically assess the detainees at the TDF for release or transfer per applicable regulations. The JIDC commander, with the advice of the assigned HUMINT and counterintelligence personnel, should provide recommendations to ensure that detainees are not transferred to another detention facility while they are still being exploited for intelligence. Recommendations for transfer or release will be coordinated with other USG departments and agencies as appropriate and forwarded to SecDef, or SecDef's designee, for decision.

13. Release to Established Recognized National Authority, Allied Facilities, or Inter-Service Agencies

a. The permanent or temporary release of detainees from the custody of US forces to the host nation, other multinational forces, or any non-DOD USG entity, requires the approval of SecDef, or SecDef's designee. The permanent or temporary release of a detainee to a foreign nation may be governed by bilateral agreements, or may be based on ad hoc arrangements. However, detainees may only be released IAW the requirements of the applicable US law, the law of war, and US policy.

b. The DFC, IAW applicable procedures, will make the transfer of a detainee from a collection point or a detention facility. All proposed transfers should be reviewed by the legal adviser to ensure compliance with applicable law and policy. Unless prohibited by command policies, immediate release of detainees may be made at the point of capture based on the decision of the most senior official on the ground. The decision should be based on criteria established by higher headquarters.

c. The temporary transfer of detainees from one facility to another is authorized to accommodate surges in the detainee population beyond capacity. Transfers will also occur to ensure detainee treatment and conditions are IAW applicable law and policy. As a general rule, detainees should not be transferred closer to military operations.

d. A detainee who is captured or detained by the US military or other agencies will be turned over to the US detention facility designated by the JFC at the earliest opportunity. Inter-Service or intratheater transfers will be executed following initial classification and administrative processing.

14. Transfer Between Department of Defense Facilities

a. Reclassification or other situations may result in a detainee's transfer. The transferring unit will determine appropriate security measures based on the type of detainee being transferred, the mode of transportation used, and other relevant conditions.

b. The DFC will:

(1) Publish a transfer order and inform the TDRC/NDRC of the movement.

(2) Verify the accuracy and completeness of the detainee's personal records and provide copies of the records (in a sealed envelope) to the guards accompanying the movement.

(3) Verify that the detainees possess their authorized clothing and equipment.

(4) Account for and prepare impounded personal property for shipment with the escorting unit or separate shipment as appropriate.

(5) Brief escort personnel on their duties and responsibilities, including procedures for an escape, a death, or other emergencies.

(6) Provide rations and basic needs to the detainees during the movement.

(7) Ensure the detainees are manifested by name, ISN, nationality, and physical condition (including a statement of "communicable diseases," if applicable).

(8) Prepare paperwork in English and other languages (if required) before transferring the detainees.

(9) Ensure detainees are given a full physical, instructions for medication, and a supply of medications.

(10) Ensure all appropriate health and disciplinary records accompany the detainee.

(11) Coordinate prior to transfer with JFC subordinate commanders regarding transfer of detainees.

15. Transfer or Release Mission

a. For transfer or release from within the JOA to either other detention facilities or direct release of the detainee back into the community, the following requirements should be met:

(1) Publish the transfer/release order informing the detainees of their impending transfer or release when required by the applicable Geneva Convention so that they may notify their next-of-kin of their new location. Caution should be exercised to ensure sensitive detainee information is not released to the general public or local officials.

(2) Verify the accuracy of the detainees' personnel records and provide copies (in a sealed envelope) to the transporting unit.

(3) Verify that detainees possess their authorized clothing and equipment.

(4) Account for and prepare impounded personal property for shipment with the escorting unit.

(5) Ensure logistic resources are adequate (food and water).

(6) Ensure that the detainees are manifested by name, rank/status, ISN, power served, nationality, and physical condition. Attach the manifest to the original receipt and provide a copy to the NDRC.

(7) Prepare paperwork in English and other languages (if required) before transferring/releasing the detainees.

(8) Coordinate, prior to transfer, with JFC subordinate commanders regarding transfer of detainees.

(9) Verify collected biometric data.

b. For release from a long-term detention facility, the following requirements should be considered. SecDef, or SecDef's designee, will send official notification of release from long-term detention. Applicable execute orders approved by appropriate authority will delineate the responsibilities and procedures to undertake. Figure IV-1 outlines the release process, from long-term detention, for detainees. The DFC may tailor stations to meet the current situation and conditions. Some steps normally taken to execute the order include:

(1) The releasing unit prepares, maintains, and reports the chain of custody and transfer/release documentation IAW current transfer and release procedures as directed by SecDef or SecDef's designee.

(2) Individual detainee preparation including, at a minimum, segregation and out-briefing, medical screening, and execution of conditional release statement for those detainees being released.

Transfer Accountability Measures

	Actions

Control and accountability	Maintain control and accountability until releases or transfers are received by the appropriate authorities.
	
	Maintain a manifest that contains:
	   Name
	   Rank/status
	   Internment serial number
	   Power served/nationality
	   Physical condition
	
	Note: A manifest is used as an official receipt of transfer and becomes a permanent record to ensure accountability of each detainee until release.

Records	Ensure that copies of appropriate personnel, finance, and medical record narrative summaries accompany released detainees. Signed release agreements will be maintained within the Department of Defense. Transfer the records to the designated receiving authority.
Personal property	Ensure that confiscated personal property (that can be released) accompanies released detainees. Conduct an inventory and identify discrepancies. Ensure that detainees sign property receipts. Ensure released detainee is provided with appropriate food, clothing, and equipment for safe transition and movement upon release.

Figure IV-1. Transfer Accountability Measures

(3) Determination of receipt/transfer location.

(4) Movement routes to transfer location. Coordinate all routes through the appropriate CCDRs.

(5) Due to operational security concerns, only make public notification of a release and/or transfer in consultation and coordination with OSD.

APPENDIX A
DETAINEE REPORTING SYSTEM

1. Introduction

The DRS is the mandated detainee accountability database for all DOD components. Key functions of the DRS at the TDF include assigning ISNs; documenting detainee transfers, releases, and reparations; recording detainee deaths; and recording detainee escapes. Timely and accurate reporting is critical to ensuring accountability of detainees and adherence to obligations under applicable US law, the law of war, and DOD policy. As detainees are collected and processed, applicable law and policy require that such information is forwarded to the appropriate authorities. The DRS creates biometrically linked official detainee records for the DOD and the USG. The DRS is a web-based system that allows for real-time data sharing with deployed systems via independent satellite communication packages. The DRS is an essential tool for detainee operations that is used to issue Geneva Convention required ISNs, and to collect and submit biometric fingerprints and photos with biographic information, including medical and property files, on all detainees.

2. National Detainee Reporting Center

The NDRC is designated by the Office of the Provost Marshal General as the recipient and archive for all detainee information. The NDRC's principal responsibility is to ensure the collection, storage, and appropriate dissemination of detainee information as required by AR 190-8/OPNAVINST 3461.6/AFI 31-304/MCO 3461.1, *Enemy Prisoners of War, Retained Personnel, Civilian Internees and Other Detainees,* and DODD 2310.01E, *The Department of Defense Detainee Program.* The NDRC provides detainee information to the ICRC to fulfill the requirements of applicable law and policy. The NDRC directs the development of the DRS, and the NDRC communicates assistance to the TDRCs when TDRCs are in use in a theater of operation. When TDRCs are not present, the NDRC will communicate assistance directly to the detention facilities. It will provide initial and replacement block ISN assignments to organizations operating in the theater. The ISN is the sole number used to track detainees and their property. The NDRC will issue a block of ISNs to organizations that process detainees upon authorization from the Provost Marshal General in conjunction with the OSD (Detainee Policy). Upon being issued an ISN, the NDRC submits the required identifiers to the DOD Biometrics Enabled Watch List Manager for review and appropriate handling of information.

3. Theater Detainee Reporting Center

The TDRC functions as the field operations agency for the NDRC. It reports all detainee data directly to the NDRC. It is the central agency responsible for maintaining information on all detainees and their personal property within an operational area. It will obtain and store information concerning all detainees in the custody of US Armed Forces and those captured by US Armed Forces and transferred to or from other powers for detention (either temporarily or permanently). The TDRC serves as the theater repository for information pertaining to accountability of detainees and implementation of DOD policy.

a. All locations issued ISNs by the NDRC will forward information concerning the detainees back to the TDRC. The ISN is used throughout the detainees' detention as their primary means of identification and is used to link the detainee with biometric data (fingerprints, facial photos, iris images, DNA), personal property, medical information, and issued equipment.

b. Any location that holds detainees may receive a DRS if deemed necessary by the CCDR, TDRC, or NDRC. All locations with DRS must conform to all reporting requirements established by the NDRC. If provided with a DRS, the facility can request ISNs (except collection points) from the TDRC and forward all information concerning the detainees to the TDRC. The ISN issued at the facility will be used throughout the detainees' detention.

APPENDIX B
DETAINEE OPERATIONS AT SEA

1. It may be necessary to detain individuals on naval vessels in situations in which they are initially captured at sea (e.g., counter-piracy operations, directed maritime interdiction operations, or recovery of shipwrecked enemy personnel in an armed conflict). Such individuals may be held on board as operational needs dictate, pending a reasonable opportunity to transfer them to a shore facility or to another vessel for eventual transfer to a shore facility. Additionally, individuals *not* initially detained at sea may be held on board naval vessels while being transported between land facilities or in other cases dictated by operational necessity. In all cases of detention at sea, detained individuals will be moved from the vessel to a shore detention facility at the earliest opportunity consistent with operational imperatives.

2. As with any detained personnel, US forces conducting at-sea detention are obligated to comply with all applicable legal and policy standards for the treatment of detainees. These include the requirement to treat detained individuals humanely and IAW Common Article 3 of the 1949 Geneva Conventions during non-international armed conflict, the Detainee Treatment Act, the principles set forth in Article 75 of Additional Protocol I to the Geneva Conventions during international armed conflict, and applicable provisions of the 1949 Geneva Convention Relative to the Treatment of Prisoners of War for EPWs.

3. Prolonged detention of captured individuals on board naval vessels is permissible only under strictly limited circumstances. Shipboard detention is therefore only a temporary measure permitted until the detained individuals can be transferred to a shore-based facility. It is limited to the minimum period necessary to transfer detainees from a zone of hostilities or as a result of operational necessity.

4. Individuals detained in connection with international armed conflict and classified as EPWs (including RP) are subject to special rules which may limit the discretion of US forces to detain such persons at sea. Article 22 of the 1949 G, provides, in pertinent part, that "Prisoners of war may be interned only in premises located on land and affording every guarantee of hygiene and healthfulness." While *temporary* at-sea detention as discussed above is not necessarily inconsistent with this prohibition, prolonged detention of detainees entitled to EPW status on board naval vessels violates US obligations under international law if such detention constitutes "internment." Under no circumstances should naval (or other) vessels be used for this purpose. The use of immobilized vessels for even temporary holding of EPWs or RP is prohibited without SecDef approval.

5. Commanders should seek assistance from legal advisors regarding the status and treatment of persons detained on board naval (or other) vessels.

Intentionally Blank

APPENDIX C
DETENTION FACILITY RIOT CONTROL MEASURES

1. Introduction

Riot control tactics, techniques, and procedures are usually written for quelling civil disturbances that occur in large open areas where the size of the responding force or the type of formation employed is not hampered by a lack of space. However, in a detention facility, detainee disturbances may occur in small, closed areas, such as a housing area, a dining facility, or a chapel where available maneuver space limits the size of the element and equipment that may be employed. The layout of each facility is different and presents its own problems when employing riot control measures.

2. Crowd Tactics Within a Detention Facility

a. In detention facility disturbances, detainees may employ a number of tactics to resist, exert control, or achieve their goals. Nonviolent tactics range from obscene remarks, taunts, and jeers, to building barricades to impede troop movement. Violent tactics used by detainees can include physical attacks on guards, other detainees, or property. The use of makeshift weapons against individuals (guards or detainees), property, or facilities is limited only by the ingenuity of the detainees, and the materials available to them.

b. The Guard Force is susceptible to violent crowd behavior. Guards will likely become emotionally stimulated during any confrontation with detainees. To counteract the effect of crowd behavior on the guard force, commanders should institute rigorous training and firm and effective leadership. This training should include a complete awareness and understanding of the use of force as well as the commander's intent.

3. Planning

DFCs must be aware of the potential risks involved in quelling disturbances within a detention facility. Careful planning minimizes collateral damage and risks to control force members. Planners must consider:

a. The location of the disturbance.

b. The estimated number of rioters.

c. Access to weapons or improvised weapons.

d. Detainees' military training.

e. Hostage situations.

4. Use of Force Guidelines

Plans, SOPs, and other directives must establish the procedures for authorization and use of lethal and nonlethal force, including riot control agents. Use of riot control agents must be approved for use by appropriate authority IAW applicable rules for the use of force. Commanders should coordinate with the staff judge advocate prior to incorporating any of the use of force guidelines in plans, SOPs, and similar directives.

5. Record of Events

A record of events must be initiated to provide a basis for the preparation and submission of a formal report to higher headquarters. Augment the record with video or still photographs if possible.

6. Training and Equipment

Guard units and associated teams must establish a continuous training program and train regularly on emergency plans, riot control formations, use of force, first aid, and interpersonal communication skills. Recommended basic riot gear used by the control force includes:

  a. Riot baton.

  b. Riot shield.

  c. Helmet with face shield and neck protection.

  d. Groin protector.

  e. Ballistic- and stab-resistant vest.

  f. Leather gloves.

  g. Shin protection.

  h. 12-gauge and 40-millimeter nonlethal munitions.

  i. Nonlethal "Stingball" hand grenade.

7. Forced Cell Move Teams

The intent of a forced cell move or extraction is to move an unruly and/or uncooperative detainee from one cell to another in a controlled manner. A forced cell move must be thoroughly planned, rehearsed, and properly resourced to ensure the safety of the team members and the detainee.

APPENDIX D
REFERENCES

The development of JP 3-63 is based upon the following primary references:

1. General

Public Law 109-163, *The Detainee Treatment Act of 2005.*

2. Multinational Treaties

a. *Geneva Convention for the Amelioration of the Condition of the Wounded and Sick in Armed Forces in the Field,* 12 August 1949.

b. *Geneva Convention for the Amelioration of the Condition of the Wounded, Sick, and Shipwrecked Members of Armed Forces at Sea,* 12 August 1949.

c. *Geneva Convention Relative to the Treatment of Prisoners of War,* 12 August 1949.

d. *Geneva Convention Relative to the Protection of Civilian Persons in Time of War,* 12 August 1949.

3. Department of Defense Publications

a. DHE-M 3301.001, *Defense Human Intelligence (HUMINT) Enterprise Manual, Volume I: Collection Requirements, Reporting, and Evaluation Procedures.*

b. DODD 1325.04, *Confinement of Military Prisoners and Administration of Military Correctional Programs and Facilities.*

c. DODD 2310.01E, *The Department of Defense Detainee Program.*

d. DODD 2311.01E, *DOD Law of War Program.*

e. DODD 3115.09, *DOD Intelligence Interrogations, Detainee Debriefings, and Tactical Questioning.*

f. DODD 3115.13, *Department of Defense Support to the High-Value Detainee Interrogation Group (HIG).*

g. DODI 1325.07, *Administration of Military Corrections Facilities and Clemency and Parole Authority.*

h. DODI 2310.08E, *Medical Program Support for Detainee Operations.*

i. DODI 3115.10E, *Intelligence Support to Personnel Recovery.*

4. Chairman of the Joint Chiefs of Staff Publications

   a. CJCSI 3290.01D, *Program for Detainee Operations.*

   b. CJCSI 5810.01D, *Implementation of the DOD Law of War Program.*

   c. JP 2-01.2, *Counterintelligence and Human Intelligence Support in Joint Operations.*

   d. JP 3-13.2, *Military Information Support Operations.*

   e. JP 3-50, *Personnel Recovery.*

5. Multi-Service Publications

   a. AR 190-8/OPNAVINST 3461.6/AFI 31-304/MCO 3461.1, *Enemy Prisoners of War, Retained Personnel, Civilian Internees and Other Detainees.*

   b. FM 5-34/MCRP 3-17A, *Engineer Field Data.*

6. United States Army Publications

   a. AR 25-1, *Information Management Army Information Technology.*

   b. AR 27-10, *Military Justice.*

   c. AR 190-47, *The Army Corrections System.*

   d. FM 2-22.2, *Counterintelligence.*

   e. FM 2-22.3, *Human Intelligence Collector Operations.*

   f. FM 3-63, *Detainee Operations.*

   g. Army Technical Publication 4-02.46, *Army Health Support to Detainee Operations.*

7. United States Air Force Publications

   a. AFI 31-117, *Arming and Use of Force by Air Force Personnel.*

   b. AMC Detainee Movement Standard Operating Procedures.

8. United States Navy Publications

   a. Secretary of the Navy Instruction 1640.9C *Department of the Navy Corrections Manual.*

   b. Navy Warfare Publication 3-07.4M, *Maritime Counter Drug and Alien Migrant Interdiction Operations.*

c. Office of the Chief of Naval Operations Instruction 1640.9A, *Guide for the Operation and Administration of Detention Facilities.*

9. Other Publications

a. United States European Command Directive 45-1, *Law of War Program.*

b. Allied JP 2.5, *Captured Persons, Materiel, and Documents.*

c. STP 21-24-SMCT, *Soldier's Manual of Common Tasks.*

d. Bagram Standard Operating Procedures.

e. Guantanamo Bay Standard Operating Procedures.

f. Guantanamo Bay Medical Standard Operating Procedures.

g. Guantanamo Bay Tiger Team Standard Operating Procedures.

Intentionally Blank

APPENDIX E
ADMINISTRATIVE INSTRUCTIONS

1. User Comments

Users in the field are highly encouraged to submit comments on this publication to: Joint Staff J-7, Deputy Director, Joint Education and Doctrine, ATTN: Joint Doctrine Analysis Division, 116 Lake View Parkway, Suffolk, VA 23435-2697. These comments should address content (accuracy, usefulness, consistency, and organization), writing, and appearance.

2. Authorship

The lead agent for this publication is the US Army. The Joint Staff doctrine sponsor for this publication is the Director for Operations (J-3).

3. Supersession

This publication supersedes JP 3-63, *Detainee Operations,* 20 May 2008.

4. Change Recommendations

a. Recommendations for urgent changes to this publication should be submitted:

TO: JOINT STAFF WASHINGTON DC//J7-JED//

b. Routine changes should be submitted electronically to the Deputy Director, Joint Education and Doctrine, ATTN: Joint Doctrine Analysis Division, 116 Lake View Parkway, Suffolk, VA 23435-2697, and info the lead agent and the Director for Joint Force Development, J-7/JED.

c. When a Joint Staff directorate submits a proposal to the CJCS that would change source document information reflected in this publication, that directorate will include a proposed change to this publication as an enclosure to its proposal. The Services and other organizations are requested to notify the Joint Staff J-7 when changes to source documents reflected in this publication are initiated.

5. Distribution of Publications

Local reproduction is authorized and access to unclassified publications is unrestricted. However, access to and reproduction authorization for classified JPs must be IAW DOD Manual 5200.01, Volume 1, *DOD Information Security Program: Overview, Classification, and Declassification,* and DOD Manual 5200.01, Volume 3, *DOD Information Security Program: Protection of Classified Information.*

6. Distribution of Electronic Publications

a. Joint Staff J-7 will not print copies of JPs for distribution. Electronic versions are available on JDEIS Joint Electronic Library Plus (JEL+) at https://jdeis.js.mil/jdeis/index/jsp (NIPRNET) and http://jdeis.js.smil.mil/jdeis/index.jsp (SIPRNET), and on the JEL at http://www.dtic.mil/doctrine (NIPRNET).

b. Only approved JPs are releasable outside the combatant commands, Services, and Joint Staff. Release of any classified JP to foreign governments or foreign nationals must be requested through the local embassy (Defense Attaché Office) to DIA, Defense Foreign Liaison PO-FL, Room 1E811, 7400 Pentagon, Washington, DC 20301-7400.

c. JEL CD-ROM. Upon request of a joint doctrine development community member, the Joint Staff J-7 will produce and deliver one CD-ROM with current JPs. This JEL CD-ROM will be updated not less than semi-annually and when received can be locally reproduced for use within the combatant commands, Services, and combat support agencies.

GLOSSARY
PART I—ABBREVIATIONS AND ACRONYMS

AFI	Air Force instruction
AFME	Armed Forces Medical Examiner
AR	Army regulation
BSC	behavioral science consultant
C2	command and control
CAT	category
CCDR	combatant commander
CDO	commander, detainee operations
CI	civilian internee
CJCSI	Chairman of the Joint Chiefs of Staff instruction
DCP	detainee collection point
DD	Department of Defense form
DFC	detention facility commander
DHA	detainee holding area
DHE-M	Defense Human Intelligence Enterprise-manual
DOD	Department of Defense
DODD	Department of Defense directive
DODI	Department of Defense instruction
DRS	detainee reporting system
EPW	enemy prisoner of war
FM	field manual (Army)
GC	Geneva Convention Relative to the Protection of Civilian Persons in Time of War
GPW	Geneva Convention Relative to the Treatment of Prisoners of War
GWS	Geneva Convention for the Amelioration of the Condition of the Wounded and Sick in Armed Forces in the Field
HUMINT	human intelligence
IAW	in accordance with
ICRC	International Committee of the Red Cross
IO	information operations
IRC	information-related capability
ISN	internment serial number

J-2X	joint force counterintelligence and human intelligence staff element
JFC	joint force commander
JFS	joint force surgeon
JIDC	joint interrogation and debriefing center
JOA	joint operations area
JP	joint publication
MCO	Marine Corps order
MI	military intelligence
MISO	military information support operations
MP	military police (Army and Marine)
NDRC	National Detainee Reporting Center
NGO	nongovernmental organization
OPNAVINST	Chief of Naval Operations instruction
OSD	Office of the Secretary of Defense
RP	retained personnel
SecDef	Secretary of Defense
SOP	standard operating procedure
TDF	theater detention facility
TDRC	theater detainee reporting center
USG	United States Government

custody. 1. The responsibility for the control of, transfer and movement of, access to, and maintenance of accountability for weapons and components. 2. Temporary restraint of a person. 3. The detention of a person by lawful authority or process. (Approved for incorporation into JP 1-02.)

detainee. Any person captured, detained, or otherwise under the control of Department of Defense personnel. (Approved for incorporation into JP 1-02.)

detainee collection point. A facility or other location where detainees are assembled for subsequent movement to a detainee holding area. Also called **DCP.** (Approved for replacement of "detainee collecting point" and its definition in JP 1-02.)

detainee holding area. A facility or other location where detainees are administratively processed and provided custodial care pending disposition and subsequent release, transfer, or movement to a theater detention facility. Also called **DHA.** (Approved for replacement of "detainee processing station" and its definition in JP 1-02.)

detainee operations. A broad term that encompasses the capture, initial detention and screening, transportation, treatment and protection, housing, transfer, and release of the wide range of persons who could be categorized as detainees. (Approved for inclusion in JP 1-02.)

National Detainee Reporting Center. The national-level center that accounts for all persons who pass through the care, custody, and control of the Department of Defense and that obtains and stores information concerning detainees and their confiscated personal property. Also called **NDRC.** (Approved for replacement of "national detainee reporting center" and its definition in JP 1-02.)

prisoner of war camp. None. (Approved for removal from JP 1-02.)

reportable incident. Any suspected or alleged violation of Department of Defense policy or of other related orders, policies, procedures or applicable law, for which there is credible information. (JP 1-02. SOURCE: JP 3-63)

retained personnel. Detainees who fall into one of the following categories: a. Designated enemy medical personnel and medical staff administrators who are exclusively engaged in either the search for, collection, transport, or treatment of the wounded or sick, or the prevention of disease; b. Staff of National Red Cross and Red Crescent Societies and that of other volunteer aid societies, duly recognized and authorized by their governments to assist medical service personnel of their own armed forces, provided they are exclusively engaged in the search for, or the collection, transport or treatment of wounded or sick, or in the prevention of disease, and provided that the staff of such societies are subject to military laws and regulations; c. Chaplains attached to enemy armed forces. Also called **RP.** (Approved for incorporation into JP 1-02.)

segregation. In detainee operations, the removal of a detainee from other detainees and their environment for legitimate purposes unrelated to interrogation, such as when necessary for the movement, health, safety, and/or security of the detainee, the detention facility, or its personnel. (JP 1-02. SOURCE: JP 3-63)

tactical questioning. The field-expedient initial questioning for information of immediate tactical value of a captured or detained person at or near the point of capture and before the individual is placed in a detention facility. Also called **TQ.** (Approved for incorporation into JP 1-02.)

theater detainee reporting center. The field operating agency of the National Detainee Reporting Center responsible for maintaining information on all detainees and their personal property within a theater of operations or assigned area of operations. Also called **TDRC.** (Approved for incorporation into JP 1-02.)